The Beginning

Manchester City – 2011/12 Premi
for ruining the end of this book).

It's a nice feeling. Champion. City had destroyed our beautiful game in style, and somehow managed to win friends in the process, due to the unique way that "typical City" never truly dies.

The story of the season couldn't have been scripted better. The controversy that has followed City around since the day of their most recent takeover has ensured that the recollection of the last manic few years can be told with barely a match report in sight. Last season was no different. From drug bans to playing bans, from striking strikers to moody Mario, from record derby wins to Joey Barton's sins, there were fireworks at every turn.

So do we still experience a "typical City"? Well not really. The current squad don't adhere or even know about the tragi-comic history of our club, and its ability to snatch defeat from the jaws of victory. And to work out when City finally shook off this tag, you have to go back to last season, and the first trophy of a generation. So it's only fitting that I start with a blog I wrote after City had lifted the FA Cup. It was a blog I had waited a long time to write.

Steve
Happy Christmas
All My Love
li x
12/12

How It Felt To See My Team Win Their First Ever Trophy

At some time around 5:15pm, on Saturday 14th May 2011, Carlos Tevez, captain of Manchester City Football Club, climbed the Wembley steps, shook a few hands, and held the FA Cup aloft. The blue moon had finally risen. City had won their first trophy since 1976. After 30 years of supporting my team, I had witnessed a City player lifting a trophy. It barely seemed real.

The last time City won a cup, I had just spoken my first words, and just learnt to walk. On 28th February 1976, the Four Seasons topped the charts with December '63. Abba's Mamma Mia had recently lost its place at the top. It was the days of terraces, rag and bone men, the Football Pink, the hottest summer ever and the first commercial Concorde flight. Margaret Thatcher had taken over the Tory party, but was 3 years away from becoming Prime Minister (remember her?). Elvis Presley was still alive too.

A lot has happened in those 12,858 days. In the period since then, Heath Ledger was born, and died. Computers took over our lives, we got something called global warming and Britain fought over the future of the Falklands, Kuwait, Iraq, and Afghanistan. I still haven't swum with dolphins.

Thirty five years and we're still here? One hundred and five domestic trophies were handed out to top-division sides in that time. A few European trophies too. I always console myself with the thought that if City had had the success of United, by now I'd be bankrupt and in the Betty Ford clinic. Small mercies and all that.

The 20th century gave us three historic moments of jaw-dropping poor predictions – Neville Chamberlain declaring peace in our time, the man who said computers would never catch on, and Peter Swales, sat in his seat in the early days of his chairmanship of Manchester City saying "this is easy".

Easy it was not. One of my first memories was relegation – a fitting way to start my lifelong relationship, my only one. David Pleat skipped across the Maine Road turf, and a generation of disappointment had begun. We went down, we came back up, we went down and further down, we came up and further up, we contested a Full Members Cup Final the day after a Manchester Derby, we had a few days in the sun, but many more in the rain, and we never sat at the top table, and we never won a trophy. This was the team that managed to get relegated on my birthday. Twice.

The stats for the last three decades make for grim reading. It can come as little surprise that City are the best supported team never to have played in the Champions League. And the list of teams that had played in a cup final since City last did was the ultimate stark reminder of their prolonged failure. The list of teams that had reached a semi-final since City last did (special shout out to Chesterfield) was almost too depressing to read.

I always used to think it was hope that kept a football fan going. The good times that may be just around the corner. But it is the hope that got ultimately destroyed time and time again, until harbouring hope seemed pointless.

As John Cleese's character Brian Stimpson said in the film Clockwise: *"It's not the despair Laura. I can take the despair. It's the hope I can't stand."*

And it's even harder to stand when the team down the road are hoovering up every trophy in sight.

Hope was a dangerous thing to have as a City fan, as it was always dashed. A quarter final at home to West Ham springs to mind, when our name was "on the cup" before defeat left us in familiar territory.

You don't support a team to win trophies, unless you are a glory hunter, but if I had known in 1982 that I wouldn't see my team win a trophy for the next 30 years, I'd have probably changed my allegiance there and then. I have never regretted my choice though. No trophies perhaps, but so many good memories, and so many good friends made in the unique family that is a football club, any football club.

I spent Saturday with many of those friends, from 5am to 4am the following day. Many cried at full time. A couple welled up just from listening to Abide With Me. The pressure of being favourites weighed heavily on many, the pressure to break the barren spell was greater. The release of that pressure at full time, the release of three decades of tension, broken promises, false hopes and near-constant dejection was immense.

When you wait so long for success, when 18 managers have passed through the door, it is inevitable that not everyone made it. Friends and family have passed away before they had the chance to see a City captain lifting up a piece of silver. They never experienced the feeling I had on Saturday afternoon. I wish I could believe they are looking down on us celebrating too, but I can't. To absent friends, to those that missed this moment, to those that never saw their football team win a trophy, it was undoubtedly for you.

A lot of blues spoke before and afterwards of those that are no longer with us. How they would have loved the game, how they would have spent the day together, how much one game of football meant to them, how they would have loved one more day together to experience what we did at the weekend.

Because days like Saturday are the epitome of what football means to people. Football is not just about the results on the pitch, it is way, way more than that. It is a family, a lifelong affiliation. Saturday showed that. Soppy perhaps, but so very true. That is why Tony Pulis wanted to win the game for his mother who passed away last year. That is why so many wanted their team to win, for parents who no longer stood by their side.

This is how it devours peoples' lives, affects their every mood, shapes who they are. Loyalties are passed from father to son (though not in my case, my father being a United fan!), from generation to generation, memories are passed on too.

Football is used as pointers for your life. This stupid game of 22 men kicking a pig's bladder (sorry, synthetic substitute) around a piece of grass has so much to answer for, but so much to give. It is because football fans invest so much time, effort and emotion into their clubs that sometimes it almost matters too much. You are a hostage to your club's fortunes. All you can do is prey and hope. Even atheists like me have preyed a thousand times in a football ground.

And credit to Stoke fans for staying at the end to support their team, to savour the day for every moment it offered to them, despite the result. I'm not sure I could have done the same. They were a pleasure to spend the day with, unlike the previous round. And credit to Tony Pulis for taking a second Wembley defeat to Manchester City with grace and dignity. They have a European adventure ahead of them, and they will love every minute of it.

Many in the press wrote about how City's day would be overshadowed by United winning the league. Their ignorance is laughable. No one spoke of United, and no one cared. Everything rested on our result, everything.

Of course the inevitable recriminations about City buying success have continued, and I am not about to revisit the tedious arguments over how to do things the right way. The fans are now labelled as arrogant, but they are the same friends that were travelling to Lincoln and watching Bury beat us at home just 12 or 13 years ago. Our current owners have run our club with as much class, dignity and thought for the fans as any other owner in my lifetime. Next year my season ticket will cost £460, and tickets for domestic cup ties will be capped at £15 until the quarter-finals. I have never been prouder of my club, its players or its owners. And irrelevant of the money, Roberto Mancini and Yaya Toure will be club legends forever. They have earned it.

So the monkey is off City's back. A new and exciting journey begins, and it seems City didn't kill football after all. Fancy that.

It was a weight off my shoulders to know City had secured
their first trophy. It took a while to take it all in to be honest.
But with a trophy under our belts, the summer dragged, with
little else to occupy us other than the constant transfer
speculation and the "in-the-knowers". It all soon became
tiresome. Whilst many with information were (and are)
genuine, with inside knowledge from a particular club, many a
fake popped up on message boards and Twitter. There was
always a set theme with your average ITK'er, so I wrote a
guide on how anyone could become one.

How To Become An ITKer

They're everywhere. They say that in England you're never
more than six feet away from a rat. Similarly, if you log onto
any football site, you're never more than six seconds from
seeing an update from an "in-the-knower".
Some people foolishly used to think that to be an in-the-
knower, you had to like, know stuff. How ridiculous. This is not
necessary at all – and with a few simple steps, you too could
be one within a couple of weeks, and have thousands of
desperate football fans hanging off your every word.
1. Set up accounts on the relevant football message boards,
and on Twitter.
2. User name is important here. On twitter "in the know" could
be used somewhere in the name, or you could take an
alternative approach and use footyagent64, footballspy1 or
something similar. Anything that suggests that you are
important, and have got news to dispense. In the know

suggests a wind-up merchant immediately, but football fans just can't help themselves. It's like moths to a light bulb, they're hooked. Even if everything you say is rubbish, it might be entertaining rubbish.

3. You now have to gain people's trust. This is the most difficult part. If you are patient you could spend time building these accounts with innocent posts that gain trust in those that read them, and save yourself for the following transfer window. This takes dedication. Whatever you decide, you must start gently, before building up momentum. It is essential though that you get off on the right foot – so best to start with some rumours that you are confident in and are this probably easily available already – but embellish the information with some wishy-washy details that make you look like you've got the inside track without committing yourself to being exposed further down the line.

Example: Lets say Nasri wants to go to Manchester United, and this is fairly common knowledge.

You write: *Nasri definitely keen to go to Old Trafford as his first option. Meetings planned with Wenger hopefully this week, but Wenger is known to be adamant he won't sell to United. Initial bid expected of £20m from United, who are reluctant to bid any higher for player with only year left on contract. Ferguson known to have given up on Sanchez or Modric, unless there is a sudden change in circumstances. Nasri now main target for Ferguson, but he is keeping watch on other players as a fall-back.*

4. Follow reliable people on Twitter, and do some surfing to sniff out information – then when presenting as your own, it might be information not yet widely available, and if it comes to pass, it makes you look genuine.

5. You might want to take one early "all-or-nothing" gamble that will destroy your credibility or cement your position for good. Take a leap of faith, an educated guess, call it what you want, and make a bold prediction. Remember, if it doesn't come off, you can always salvage your reputation with the age-old excuse of terms not being agreed, problems over fees, etc.

6. Vagueness is the key. After all, you need to protect your sources, who go right to the top. You can dispense endless rumours without actually saying much at all (see example above). You are aware of discussions on a number of players becoming more advanced this week at Arsenal. Your sources tell you Manchester United are looking at sealing a loan deal for one of their unwanted players, but negotiations have hit a few snags, but hopeful of conclusion by end of next week or soon after.

7. Throw in a few titbits about signings for lower-league teams. Most won't check if news was already common knowledge, or even true.

8. Occasionally post at 4am in the morning, giving the impression you are sealing an important deal in Kuala Lumpur.

9. Occasionally post that you have no new news, no new information, and that things are "quiet". This will make you appear more genuine.

10. Have your excuses ready. So you said there was no new news at Manchester City ten minutes before they announced the signing of Xavi? Don't panic, you can get round this. There's an excuse for every occasion.

Example post: *Xavi signing admittedly taken me by surprise. Heard rumblings last week that deal was a possibility, but source said not to mention it as negotiations at critical point – clearly they have kept very tight counsel on this, to ensure move went through. Great signing by City. More news as I get it.*

11. If you are truly found out, burn your bridges. Delete what you can, bury your head in the sand and deny having ever made the comments. Claim you have been misquoted. A long period of silence will ensure most people will forget what you have said in past, and you can return with a clean slate.

12. A good tactic on a message board is to make it clear you are NOT an in-the-knower, but simply passing on good information. This apparent modesty will gain trust.

13. If you're well established as being in the know, you are allowed a mistake. In fact, you're allowed a hundred, there will still be people who will seek out your posts eagerly.

14. Another option: find someone who actually is "in-the-know" and just use their information. But subtly.

15. Deadline day – this is YOUR day, a day of wild speculation, manic developments and last-gasp deals before an autumn hibernation. Until Big Ben goes bong at 5pm, the world is your oyster. Go for it. As clubs are often desperate at this point and try any number of deals unsuccessfully, you might as well throw around plenty of wild rumours. No one will really know whether they were made up.

16. September, October, November, December, February, March, April, and a bit of May. A time for silence? Far from it. These are the most fruitful months of all for an "in-the-knower". No deals can be done now, but plans can be made, so you can make claims without being proved wrong.

17. Everything else is up to you. Perhaps settle on one team, claiming to have a source within the club, or perhaps fling your net wider, claiming to work within the game. It can be whatever you want to be, and whatever you say, someone somewhere will believe you.

So as you can see, pretty easy. Just a few hours gets you started, and before long you can have the adoration of thousands. I'm not sure why you would, but it seems plenty would disagree – a feeling of power can come in many forms.

There were other things to keep us talking though – there always is with City of course. Just to spice things up, Kolo Touré decided to pick up a drugs ban, and at the time seemed to have put an end to his Manchester City career. Here's the article I wrote soon after the news broke.

Kolo Toure HAD To Be Banned

Last week, Manchester City defender Kolo Touré was banned from all football activities after being found guilty of taking a prohibited substance, contained within a dieting pill belonging to his wife. It was backdated to the date when he was initially suspended, so he will be available again in early September.

As most will be aware, it is now standard procedure for the Football Association to carry out random drug tests on players without giving clubs any notice. The actual sampling officers are independent though, and are accompanied by an FA supervising officer (a doctor or physiotherapist approved by the FA).

As a Manchester City fan, should I be outraged at such a punishment, the result of a seemingly honest mistake by a teetotal, devout Muslim? No, of course not. He deserves to be banned; in fact he HAD to be banned.

You could argue that what he took was not related to football, and not performance-enhancing. That it was an honest mistake, a stupid solitary mistake, which should not be punished so harshly. After all, everyone makes mistakes. But the fact is that he took something that is banned, and he knew what the consequences of doing this would be. All players have it drummed into them by club doctors and management that they cannot take a whole raft of medicinal products, that there is a whole swathe of ingredients that are no-go areas and that if there is any doubt with taking something they should get it checked out first. It's part of being a professional footballer.

You could even argue that by taking something to slim down, it could be considered performance enhancing. I wouldn't personally.

Toure was found to have taken a "specified substance". According to the World Anti-Doping Agency's "code", "specified substances" are those that are "more susceptible to a credible, non-doping explanation."

The code states: "If the athlete can prove that he or she did not intend to enhance performance by using them to the satisfaction of the results management authority, the sanction under the World Anti-Doping code can go from a warning to a two-year ban."

It's impossible to say what the correct ban length should be – there's no rulebook that decides the fairness of these things, it is entirely subjective. One journalist tweeted that Rio Ferdinand and Paddy Kenny got 9 months and Touré only 6 months, so where was the consistency? Yeah, because all drug offences are the same, so it should be the same punishment for everyone.

Paddy Kenny was banned for nine months in September 2009 after testing positive for ephedrine, a prohibited substance found in cold remedies. The FA chose not to punish Paddy Kenny to the full extent of its powers (the aforementioned 2 years) after admitting that he had not deliberately sought to enhance performance when taking an over-the-counter cold remedy without consulting Sheffield United's medical team, in a case thus very similar to Touré's. On the other hand, Hamilton midfielder Simon Mensing was banned for just a month after testing positive for another specified substance, methylhexaneamine, in December 2010. This too appeared to be a dietary supplement, and he provided credible evidence to support his case. The Scottish Football Association took that information into account when sentencing him to an unusually short ban, using much more leniency than if he had been up before their English counterparts. There will always be inconsistencies between different FA's, but within an FA, there will presumably be just reason for differing periods of bans for particular players.

Comment must be made too on Rio Ferdinand. It was milliseconds after the announcement of the six month ban came out that the first United fan complained about the injustice of it all. You see, in many United fans' eyes, Ferdinand didn't do anything wrong, and it is a miscarriage of justice that a player we know to have taken a banned substance gets a lesser punishment than a player we do not know to have taken a banned substance. But leaving Ferdinand out of this, let's look at the general scenario, and cut to the chase – a player who misses a drug test should get the maximum punishment available. If anyone cannot work out the logic behind this, then I suggest you go back to primary school.

But perhaps it should be explained anyway – those who decide punishments must presume that someone who missed a test is guilty of taking a banned substance, and a performance-enhancing one at that, and thus pass judgement with that assumption in mind. They must do this because if they did not, any player who had taken a banned substance and was asked to take a drugs test would deliberately miss it knowing the punishment would be less that way. Players must be aware that the test must be taken – and that not taking it will not be in their interest. It is the only logical stance to take.

As for Ferdinand, I have heard claims from United fans that the player offered to return immediately to take the test, an offer that was rejected by the drug-testers. If this is true then he has claims for unfair treatment, but I have never heard this claim mentioned in an official publication, so it's mere speculation. I've also heard claims he did do the test the day after, but still got banned. Again, if so (and I have no idea if it is), then it does seem harsh on him.

There was extra criticism in many circles to the fact that Touré's ban covers the summer months – should it not just cover months of the football season? Well it's not a new rule, but the fact remains is he will miss pre-season, so even when his ban expires in early September, he will still be nowhere ready to return to the first team. Because of this he will probably end up missing five months of playing time anyway. But it is a point worth debating – depending on which time of year a player gets banned, can alter how much football he misses.

There are reports in the newspapers at the moment that Touré is looking to appeal the decision, and hopefully get the ban reduced. If this is true then I am disappointed. There's no harm in chancing your arm I guess, but personally I would take the punishment and move on. After all, even if Touré did prove to the FA that he only ingested a prohibited substance unknowingly, his punishment according to Wada could still have been as big as a two-year ban.

Drug tests are a serious part of maintaining the integrity of the sport. Stupidity and ignorance are no excuses, and the FA's disciplinary commission rightly refuses to accept ignorance as an excuse. The best thing Touré can do is accept this and give his all on his return. He is being fully paid during his six month absence, and I would hope this should spur him on more – he made an innocent-enough mistake, but in many aspects he has been very fortunate indeed.

Whilst the subject of my greatest ever man-crush, Sergio Aguero, was making his way to our club (sorry David Silva), off the field, City were making further plans to meet Financial Fair Play rules and become self-sufficient by announcing naming rights on the City of Manchester stadium. The plans were inevitable, and had been an open secret for months - there was little surprise at the announcement. Also inevitable was the hysterical overreaction from sections of the press, as if this had never happened before, an easy excuse to have a go at City, an easy stick to beat City with. Even less surprising was my heated argument with the Guardian's chief wind-up-merchant Barry Glendenning. My article was written in a period of anger in under half an hour, and was my most read ever.

Stop The Moral Outrage Over A Sponsorship Deal

Today Manchester City announced a sponsorship deal for their stadium that means it will be named after the airline Etihad, in a deal worth up to £300m over ten years, which includes sponsorship of the area around the stadium and various other interests.

I've yet to encounter a City fan who was remotely concerned at this news – far from it, as it was greeted as a two-fingered salute to Michel Platini and his financial fair play rules. It was common knowledge anyway – news of this deal has been rumoured for many months now, it was always going to happen as part of the sheikhs' second phase of being economically self-sufficient.

Elsewhere though, there was outrage. Waving the placards most vigorously of all was the ever-entertaining Ollie Holt of the Mirror. He was depressed, distraught, devastated even at the news. Here are some of his thoughts on Twitter:

There are many ways in which the current owners of Manchester City have shown class. Renaming the stadium after a sponsor isn't one of them.

*I know part of the answer is FFP but if City have got so much cash, why do they have to **sell a piece of their soul** for stadium naming rights?*

Many City fans saying they don't care about stadium renaming because new stadium never had an identity anyway. Sad comment on the game.

Is it acceptable then to change name of team too? Presumably all in favour of Etihad Stadium would be fine with Etihad City as name of team.

Now if Maine Road had been re-named, I'd be rather more upset, as would a lot of City fans. But it hasn't. What is being re-named is an eight year old stadium that didn't have a set name anyway. How often have you heard a City fan refer to the City of Manchester Stadium? Some called it COMS, some called it Eastlands, some, like when getting a taxi to the ground, just call it "the city ground please mate". Fans call their ground various names all the time, and will continue to call their ground what they want, sponsor or no sponsor.

In fact someone argued online of the loss of heritage in changing from Eastlands to the Etihad Stadium, the irony completely lost on him that Eastlands is not, and has never been the name of the ground – but it goes to show this deal changes nothing – fans and journalists alike have been happy to spend the last eight years calling the ground by a made-up name.

So I can see how in theory a re-name could be seen as sacrilege and offensive. One journalist commented that he would be disgusted if Celtic Park was re-named. But this is different, clearly. How can everyone not see this? This is not Celtic Park, this is not Wembley, Villa Park or Anfield. If it had happened eight years earlier no one would have batted an eyelid.

It was acceptable for Arsenal to move into a sponsored stadium without having to defend themselves, and Wigan and Bolton. It's fine for Bayern Munich to do the same. Why the outrage now?

Inevitably the old misconception that Etihad actually translates to mean United was once more dug up out of the woodwork. It doesn't, and I couldn't care less if it did anyway, but if that's all people have got to attack City with, then the outlook is definitely rosy.

People can moan about the soul of a club (a ridiculous concept that is impossible determine and does not in fact exist), about modern football being all about money, about the loss of identity and so on, but the bottom line is this – the stadium naming deal makes no difference to anything. Same team, same ground, same players, same kit, same players, same division, same match-day experience, same everything.

The fact is that the deal was inevitable the moment the financial fair play plans were agreed. As I have argued before, however noble Platini's intentions were (not very, a cynic might say), the consequences of this will be clubs desperately trying to earn more money any which way they can, leading to sponsorship deals aplenty, higher ticket prices, and even less thought given to the fans. If you want to blame someone, look towards France.

Holt had already written an article on the topic a few days ago, bemoaning the re-naming of Leicester's ground, to the King Power Stadium.

"If you defile the stadium by prostituting its name, you destroy part of the experience."

No you don't Ollie. My experience next season will not be 1% worse because of the name of the stadium. Any true football fan would know this.

"I could live with the Walkers Stadium even if it was named after a bag of crisps. It was the name of Leicester's new arena and had been since they moved there from Filbert Street in 2002."

What a ridiculous argument – you can have a sponsor's name on the stadium when you move there, but don't you dare do it eight or nine years down the line, as this is removing the soul from the game, and a depressing sign of what football has become? Utter hogwash.

Much of the argument revolves around that last point – how football is run by money, how things aren't what they used to be. The fact is, there's nothing worse than nostalgia. Football when I first started watching it in the 1980's was a terrible time to be involved as a fan. Poor grounds, poor facilities, poor crowds, poor football on the whole, hooliganism, ID cards and tragedy after tragedy. I still loved every minute of course, but give me a sponsored ground and indoor toilets any day. Football has been about money since Sky invented the game in 1992. It seems some have only just woken up to the fact. Holt also mentioned Chesterfield's sponsored stadium name, blissfully unaware of the massive financial problems they have suffered over the past decade or so, and how this deal will make their future even more secure.

Regarding City, the deal goes beyond the naming of a stadium anyway. It will form part of the £1 billion regeneration of the surrounding area, one of the poorest areas of the city. It will provide world-class sporting facilities and community football pitches. Etihad will also partner on youth and community projects both locally, throughout Britain and internationally. And clubs are after all part of the community in which they exist, and there to serve it. And it should be made clear too that Manchester City council do very well financially from the football club.

So what's more important? A fatuous sense of outrage because the name of an almost new building has been changed, or the regeneration of east Manchester? Not a tough decision.

It was becoming a bore reading about criticism of City. There was even outrage (and I am not exaggerating, I assure you) in parts of the media when City announced a tie-up with EA Sports, and had the temerity to show a computer image of Nasri scoring in a Manchester derby on their website! OMG!!! What a lack of class! So tacky!!

But the transfer rumours were always the key talking point in the summer, as ever. It was inevitable that City would be linked with some big names. And it was inevitable that we would be spuriously linked with one player in particular. And so it came to pass, and this is what I wrote.......

Read All About It

The Sunday Mirror were cock-a-hoop with this week's big exclusive. Cristiano Ronaldo was considering a move to Manchester City, if a number of demands were met.

These included being paid a mere £400,000 a week, the number 7 shirt, being guaranteed the captaincy and to always be the top paid player at City. Plus he wanted a private helipad at the City of Manchester stadium, Ryan Gigg's SIM card, 200 swans in a moat at his house and a personal slave to follow him around the pitch fanning him on warm match days.

When I saw the article I was left shaking my head at the ludicrous nature of the claims. The idea that City had really sent him a picture of a Bentley covered in money was ridiculous, and as usual there were few quotes except from anonymous "sources", and all offers to him were made from mysterious third parties. Whatever, it will surely never happen whatever the truth, especially with the new financial fair play rules coming in. City cannot pay a player £400,000 a week in the same way they cannot make a £150m purchase.

The response to the rumour from City fans was fairly predictable. The idea of the world's 2nd best player (debatable, I know) coming to City seemed to appal many. There is the United connection of course, not that that has stopped City before (though the appointment of David Platt last season for example was met with a wave of opposition and anger), but it was his behaviour on the pitch and as a human being in general that seemed to put most off.

Personally I care little for whether he is the world's nicest man or an odious arrogant, perma-tanned narcissist. He is without doubt one of a select band of players who would instantly take the team onto another level. Yes, City can be successful without him, but the fact is that with him success would be far more likely.

But for many, it would be a step too far. It would cross a line about who it is and isn't acceptable to employ at the club. Don't get me wrong, I am not totally apathetic to the character of new signings. There are certain players I would never want to see at this club, whatever their worth to the team. And there's very little in the way that Ronaldo acts that endears me to him. Nor can I stand players who dive (he undoubtedly goes to ground very easily, as do a whole swathe of players nowadays), who whinge at referees, or who fancy themselves so much they burst into tears if a hair is misplaced after a crowded corner. But I could live with it. The fact is if Ronaldo had come through the ranks and was already a City player, every City fan would be defending his actions, just like United fans used to do. We are all hypocritical beasts, us football fans.

Either way, the discussion is redundant, apart from debating the hypotheticals of players you previously hated turning up at your club, as there is zero chance of Ronaldo moving to City, or anywhere else for that matter, this summer.

But what the whole story showed more than anything was how the media works – by Tuesday of this week The Sun's EXCLUSIVE was how Ronaldo had snubbed City – yep, yet again a football club was snubbed by a player that they had probably never expressed any interest in. Only last week I personally snubbed Barcelona, and last year rejected a move to AC Milan. European football correspondent Antony Kastrinakis's story about Cristiano Ronaldo turning down Manchester City's offer was of course an EXCLUSIVE!

Kastrinakis got this exclusive by basically listening to an interview on Spanish radio. Though to be honest, he probably didn't even do that.

Ideally of course I do want my club's players to behave with decorum, respect and dignity at all times. I would love a team full of Vincent Kompanys and David Silvas. Players are repsentatives of the club, they affect its image, and the mentality of players like the two mentioned above are great for team spirit and for morale, as well as making the manager's job a hundred times easier. But we are foolish to expect every player to be model professionals, as footballers have never been, and never will be good role models. I might not like him one bit, but if Cristiano Ronaldo had come to City he would never have been a club legend, but he would be welcome by me for what he would bring to the team. But the line any fan draws on who is and isn't acceptable to buy is different for all, and it is understandable why many fans want nothing to do with him.

Ridiculous rumours weren't exclusive to City though, naturally. Due to not having a life, I noted down some of the more ridiculous tabloid rumours during the summer, for a blog I wrote after the window had finally slammed shut, and had thus put us all out of our misery.

The month of May started on an appropriately crazy note, with Nigel Reo Coker's agent talking of a move to Napoli. On the 4th May, the Daily Mail reckoned that 'Jose Mourinho is ready to rival Manchester United and Liverpool in the £15m race for Ashley Young'. The Daily Star on the 6th May claimed Manchester City were to bid £30m + James Milner for Gareth Bale. The same day it was reported that Juventus wanted Ipswich striker Connor Wickham and Blackburn defender Phil Jones

Off the pitch, and on 31st May it was reported that Craig Bellamy was a leading contender to replace Dave Jones, who was sacked as Cardiff boss after the club's play-off failure according to the Daily Mail. The Guardian also declared that Bellamy was the favourite to replace Jones.

Next, came the surprise link of Jermain Defoe to Arsenal. Yeah, that was going to happen.

The next day, the Mirror said that Blackburn were after Emmanuel Adebayor, as part of a £30m spending spree. How did that go chaps?

Next, at the People, came news of Joey Barton going to Arsenal. Rumours also resurfaced about Marcus Senna going to Swansea.

On the 21st June, the Irish independent reported that Liverpool were one of five clubs after John O' Shea.

The following day, The Sun brought us news that Barcelona were planning a £27.5million bid for David Luiz.

They claimed: *'The Brazilian, signed from Benfica, has indicated he might listen to an offer from Barca, but only if Chelsea give their blessing."*

More bizarrely than that was The Daily Mail reporting that Zenit St Petersburg were considering a move for Adebayor.

On the 15th August, reports resurfaced linking Raul to Blackburn again. If you want a spurious reason for the link, read on:

'After scoring a brilliant solo goal against Cologne on Saturday, Raul made a point of not celebrating. It was being seen as a sign he could be on his way. Steve Kean is interested but has a limited budget while Malaga and Russian side Anzhi have also shown interest.'

And as for transfer deadline the day – well where would you start? The holy grail of baseless rumour-mongering, the stories flew about like confetti in the wind. The usual stuff of course of people, with people seeing Christiano Ronaldo in Manchester Airport, Raul in a chippy in Darwen, and Xavi entering in the back door of Goodison (all football stadiums have a little back door that few know about). The most ridiculous rumour on twitter was that Manchester City had bid £100m + Mario Balotelli for Lionel Messi – and that Barcelona were considering the deal. Amazingly, it never happened – I can't think why.

And at the end of it all, Samuel Eto'o is playing in Dagestan, Owen Hargreaves in the blue half of Manchester, Scott Carson is in Turkey, and Carlos Tevez is still flitting between the two restaurants of Manchester. You couldn't make it up.

What struck me most though was not the ridiculous nature of some of the speculation, which had stopped entertaining me years ago. It was more the language used when discussing players moving clubs. So I wrote something about that too.

The Language of the Transfer Window

With a mere seven weeks to go in the summer **transfer** window, things are beginning to hot up. The papers are full of potential and completed deals, managers' targets, and failed bids. But all the while, the whole process has to be explained by Her Majesty's press in a certain way. Teams don't just enquire about players, bid for them and sign them. That would be far too boring. Instead, we get what were seemingly a random set of flowery descriptions to keep the reader awake. And there seems to be a common theme running throughout.

The one thing that happens most during a transfer window is that a lot of clubs are snubbed. Teams are always being snubbed. It's just as well clubs have thick skins or they could really suffer a crisis of self-confidence. Often clubs are snubbed by a player they had never even enquired about, which seems like the cruellest of snubs. This has happened to "moneybags" **Manchester City** a lot recently. A rogue **rumour** is started up (by an agent) about their interest in someone (usually to get that player an improved contract), the player comes out to say he has no interest in joining Manchester City, and the press dutifully report it as "Player X Snubs Manchester City", despite the fact Manchester City probably have no idea who he is.

Swooped. Football clubs on the look-out for players are for some reason compared to birds of prey. Clubs appear to sit on tree branches waiting for the right moment, before swooping in on their desired player, and carrying him away in their talons. What happened to the good old days of fax machines and a courtesy phone call?

All the while, the broadcasters are trying to keep up, and pretending they are the ones in the know. A lot of the time Sky Sports News understands, which basically means Sky Sports News has been surfing the internet or reading newspapers. The BBC do this a lot too – it seems a key component of sports broadcasters is the capacity to understand stuff. Empathy, basically. Only today the BBC has published an article on the Carlos Tevez situation in which they understand a whole swathe of things.

Occasionally a team has stolen a march, which sounds like a pretty horrible thing to do, personally (and a logistical nightmare). Manchester City last week stole a march on the race to sign Samir Nasri, but as Nasri has since jetted off on Arsenal's pre-season tour, it seems the march escaped and is back where it belongs.

Players meanwhile are keen to demand "assurances". Their written contract is no longer sufficient. They want to know where the club is heading, who they are signing, and the weather for the next two years, otherwise they will have a strop and go on hunger strike until they have forced through a move to Real Madrid.

And most players seem to be described as an ACE. Or if young, they may be a STARLET (especially prevalent with young Belgian players it seems). Wigan lined to Cameroon

ACE. Scunthorpe ACE joins Millwall on loan. Belgian STARLET linked with move to Chelsea. You get the idea.

Not everyone can be an ACE or a STARLET though. Some players are described as flops. Football is full of flops. Football players don't fail, they flop. Flops are not attractive propositions in the transfer market, but flops can be resurrected, so a bargain could be had from buying a flop. Don't write off flops.

Back to the jungle, and teams are in the hunt for new players. Manchester United can sign Ashley Young, but only if they can find him. Armed with nothing more than a spear, some camouflage gear and a large net, the hunt begins….and as time passes, Sky Sports News will understand them to be closing in on their target. They make audacious moves (break-dancing?) for players they have been on the trail of, having tracked them for a while (with GPS, presumably).

Most of the news though is nothing more than speculation, normally wild (of course). Again, nature helps us out. Wild speculation is different to your common house-trained domestic speculation, as it is unpredictable, can be aggressive towards humans, and lives in a privet hedge on the outskirts of the Black Forest. Approach with caution.

Clubs eye other teams' players (across a crowded dance floor?). They pursue players (across fields in little buggies). We hear of price tags, as if players are items of clothing. Can get 20% off with your loyalty card? Clubs are known to be lining up a player (sounds like a firing squad). Or weighing up a move. Negotiations break down (hope the club are with the AA). Teams are alerted by problems with players. Players are poised to sign (try and picture the Karate Kid when he had hurt his foot so fought on one leg). Moves are hijacked by other clubs – players are presumably held on isolated airport runways until the club gets what it wants. In fact, this isn't far off what Alex Ferguson did when signing Dimitar Berbatov.

Mostly though, players are approached. I imagine a dark alleyway, long coats, and a man smoking a cheroot (or a

Gauloises if in France) sidling up to the designated player under a lamppost with a secret password. Then negotiations can begin.

Unsettled, want-away players are offered an escape route away from clubs, presumably via a secret underground tunnel. That's after issuing come-and-get-me pleas of course. This leads to a battle for the player, who edges towards a move, before finally sealing a new club.

The rest knuckle down, travel the world and post pictures on Twitter of them planking. But soon, thankfully, it will all be over, for now. Deals will be finalised, players will slip through the grasp of clubs, some players will be captured and we can all get back to watching some football and moaning about Alan Shearer on Match Of The Day. Hallelujah.

Pre-Season Bore

Pre-season has little going for it except the desperation of the football fan to see some football. But this being City, they managed to create a controversy. Naturally the villain of the piece was Mario Balotelli, who decided when through on goal to turn round and try and back-heel the ball into the net, instead stroking it wide, in a match against the LA Galaxy. Mancini was furious and subbed him immediately, a touch line spat soon ensuing. At the time I understood Mancini's anger, but I think Balotelli was hard done by - I think he genuinely thought the whistle had gone.

Elsewhere, and in the Dublin Super Cup, City eventually excelled, beating Inter Milan 3-0, which helped build anticipation for the proper football ahead.

Eventually the season was upon us. There was the small matter of the Community Shield, United grabbing a traditional last-minute winner in a match that City were rubbish in, in a match neither I nor Mancini cared one jot about.

Alan Hansen though saw the match as the the proof we all needed that United are the team to beat, and that it was their title to lose (they are defending champions, this should be obvious to him anyway). Under an article entitled: Community Shield Has Changed Everything, he added:
"Suddenly they are overwhelming favourites. They look a team of tremendous strength in depth, something that has almost come out of nowhere. They are young, vibrant, exciting. The young players who finished the game looked as though they had been at Old Trafford for years. And they are a team, something which City emphatically are not. "

But it didn't matter much at all. A last minute-winner in a pre-season friendly tells us nothing about how a nine-month campaign will pan out. From 1997 to 2004, the team that won the Community Shield didn't go on to win the league the following season but in the last 6 yrs, 5 teams have done it, reversing the trend. Statistics don't tell half the story of course. Teams that won on penalties do not provide evidence of a stronger team – such games are effectively draws, in the context of predicting league success. And City have now reversed the newest trend by clinching the title.

As is traditional, the sports fraternity all published their pre-season predictions, and there were some crackers. It's important to note the double-standards of City's coverage over the past season. We were told that with our money we should walk the league. Tony Evans at the Times said we should have had it wrapped up by Christmas, which is of course impossible. On the other hand, we were told that money doesn't guarantee success. So which one is it? After all, when it looked like City had blown the lead, huge swathes of the media called it a disaster that City had been outdone with such massive resources. How bizarre then that before the season, virtually no-one tipped us for the title. The bookies had us as third favourites.

Whatever happens in the transfer market this summer, Manchester United will once more be favourites for the title, which can come as little surprise. At 6/4 they are clear favourites ahead of Chelsea at 11/4, Manchester City at 4/1 and Arsenal at 8/1. Basically the bookies see the top 4 as remaining the same, in the same order, as last season.

And if only I had backed up my words with money....

As for top goal-scorer in the Premiership next season, the top two are both Manchester United players – Rooney, fresh from a pre-season hat trick is the favourite at 7/1, Hernandez 8-1. Torres is an unappealing 9/1, but Van Persie at 9/1 seems the most attractive if only he could stay fit.

*Relegation 4/1 for **Blackburn** is rather tempting…*

*In Italy, AC Milan are favourites for the **Serie A** title at 6/5, Inter are 13/8, but perhaps Juventus could be tempting at 6/1.*

(please note that I've edited out all my other appalling predictions…)

It's traditional at the end of any season to cry some tears of laughter at how the "experts" saw the season panning out. Predictions are a dangerous game, and we have all made some terrible ones, but some of what follows was drivel right from the start.

BBC: Only six teams featured in the predictions, and their survey found that Manchester United were the overwhelming favourites to retain their title, with only three votes going to Manchester City and one to Liverpool.

Mark Lawrenson: 1 Man Utd 2 Man City 3 Chelsea 4 Liverpool.
"Sir Alex Ferguson always gets the pre-season training right to gear United up for their traditional strong finish at the end of season. They have got a squad to cope with all the cup competitions, and the Champions League, and real competition for players and a winning mentality too. They have got the best team, the best squad and the best manager. Basically, they have got the lot."

Mark Bright: 1 Liverpool 2 Man Utd 3 Man City 4 Arsenal.
"Liverpool finished 22 points behind United last season but only Sir Alex Ferguson amassed more points than Kenny Dalglish since the 'king' took over from Roy Hodgson. Why will they win it? The Reds have four players who could grace any team in the Premier League: Pepe Reina, Steven Gerrard, Luis Suarez and Andy Carroll, then add to the mix promising

youngsters like John Flanagan, new faces like Charlie Adam and Stewart Downing plus team spirit, desire and 21 years of hurt."

Nigel Adderley: 1 Man Utd 2 Liverpool 3 Chelsea 4 Arsenal. *"I can't see beyond United winning the title again. There will be no World Cup hangover for players like Wayne Rooney this season which should help their youngsters integrate into the team. Liverpool have so much attacking flair now so Steven Gerrard should benefit from not being overburdened. Chelsea need Fernando Torres to start scoring quickly and also develop an understanding with whoever plays alongside him. Arsenal should scrape into the top four providing the Cesc Fabregas and Samir Nasri money is spent on the right areas of the team. Despite the millions lavished on their squad, I think City may miss out on the top four – rather like Tottenham last season – a decent run in the Champions League could have a negative impact on their domestic results."*

Oliver Holt (Daily Mirror) – "Charlie Adam could be the buy of the season." (a view backed up by Phil Thompson).

Paul Merson
Champions: Man Utd
Second: Chelsea
Third: Man City (but lower if Tevez goes)
Bottom three: QPR, Swansea, Norwich
Top scorer: Fernando Torres
Best buy: Charles N'Zogbia

Charlie Nicholas
Top scorer: Javier Hernandez
Best buy: David de Gea
Worst buy: Sergio Aguero isn't value for money

Over at football365.com, every writer tipped United for the title. One writer, as is obligatory, considered Aguero to be a waste of money. So close.

The Season Begins

But finally, the season was upon us. An article I wrote about the season ahead showed my uncertainty on how it would go. I don't think most people had a good idea of whether City could win the league. Most seemed to think second would be a good season. It was a team packed full of talent, but this was all new territory.

There was still time for one more rant though, before we got underway. Because throughout the constant sniping at City and their wealth, one particular lie kept cropping up in despatches. It was the typical comment made by a pea-brained keyboard warrior on Twitter, the sort of person who obtains all their information from the Daily Star, but it was something I could not ignore any longer.

The Difference Between Success & History

It's gone beyond tedious now, even beyond parody. The criticisms of Manchester City's spending was boring two years ago. Now it resembles the pathetic ramblings of a drunken spurned lover. Or a frustrated Harry Redknapp counting down the hours until he can manage his beloved England.
And what's most tedious of all? Well it's the claim that City have no history. I can't count how many times I have heard this said. And I think some people are so utterly stupid they actually believe what they say.

Javier Maschereno joined in with the stupidity a couple of years ago, claiming Manchester City had no history, a similar refrain to many on twitter incredulous last week that Sergio Aguero could choose City over someone like Liverpool. Atletico Madrid offered to match City's wages, but hey, he clearly moved for the money.

"You can buy players, but you cannot buy history," said
Mascherano. Yawn.

For the record, Manchester City beat Liverpool into being by
twelve years, to the FA Cup by 61 years, to the League Cup
by 11 years and to a European trophy by three years.

Notts County, Preston North End, and even City have histories
longer than many countries.

Here's a summary of that non-existent history. Manchester
City were founded in 1880 as St. Mark's (West Gorton) – they
became Ardwick Association Football Club in 1887 and
Manchester City in 1894. Cit y gained their first honours by
winning the Second Division in 1899; with it came promotion
to the highest level in English football, the First Division. They
went on to claim their first major honour on 23 April 1904,
beating Bolton Wanderers 1–0 at Crystal Palace to win the FA
Cup; City narrowly missed out on a League and Cup double
that season after finishing runners-up in the League. In the
seasons following the FA Cup triumph, the club was dogged
by allegations of financial irregularities, culminating in the
suspension of seventeen players in 1906, including captain
Billy Meredith, who subsequently moved across town to
Manchester United. A fire at Hyde Road destroyed the main
stand in 1920, and in 1923 the club moved to their new
purpose-built stadium at Maine Road in Moss Side, the same
year that Wembley Stadium opened.
They have won the top league in 1936-37 and in 1967-8, and
have been runners-up three times. They have won what is
now the Championship seven times, the FA Cup five times,
the League Cup twice, and the European Cup Winners' Cup
once. And so on….

Notts County meanwhile are the oldest of all the clubs in the
world that are now professional, having been formed in 1862.
County pre-dated the Football Association and initially played
a game of its own devising, rather than association football. At
the time of its formation, Notts County, like most sports teams,
were considered to be a "gentlemen-only" club. Notts County

are considered to be one of the pioneers of the modern game and are the oldest of the world's professional association football clubs (there are older professional clubs in other codes of football, and Sheffield F.C., an amateur club founded in 1857, are the oldest club now playing association football).

The club initially played at Park Hollow in the grounds of the old Nottingham Castle. In December 1864, the decision was made to play games against outside opposition, and it was decided that the club needed to find a bigger venue. After playing at several grounds, The Magpies settled at Trent Bridge Cricket Ground in 1883. In November 1872, the Notts County full-back Ernest Greenhalgh played for England against Scotland in the first-ever international match, thereby becoming the club's first international player. In 1888, Notts County, along with eleven other football clubs, became a founding member of The Football League. On 25 March 1891, Notts County reached the FA Cup final for the first time…and, well I could continue like this for the next few hours.

If you look REALLY hard, can you see a bit of a history there. Of course, Notts County haven't won the Premier League or the Champions League, or even been in the top league since football began (1992), so it's not a real history in the eyes of some. So if they were to be taken over by a billionaire, and started splashing the cash, would you begrudge them the right?

What fans who don't like upstarts spending money and disrupting the status quo mean is not that the likes of City don't have history, as they clearly do (and a relegation battle is as much a part of a club's history as a league title), but that they don't have a history of success, in recent times alone, and thus haven't earned the right to buy loads of expensive players.

So the argument is: win things, stay in the Champions league, and expand your global fan base – this is how the fans of the existing top four of the last decade or so have decided it should be done. God forbid if anyone else should try a different way.

But where is the dividing line when fans pass judgement on whether are teams are doing things the right way? What are the minimum requirements to spend lots of money and buy some of the best players in the world? Current league champions? European champions within last few years? Five trophies within last decade? Really successful twenty-five years ago so therefore got more "history" and prestige? Let's say £20m per trophy. Only fair that if you win something, you should be able to widen the gap between yourself and your competitors. No other sport in the world allows this, but apparently football has a different perception of right and wrong.

You should only be able to spend what you earn will be the comeback – but who decided it was acceptable for successful teams to earn so much more than everyone else? Why, the successful teams did of course. Of course now that City are raising revenue and announcing sponsorship deals, and thus will be spending what they earn, that has been deemed unacceptable too. But if you think the figure for City is inflated, save some ire for Real Madrid, who have signed a deal earning 5 million euros per year JUST for advertising around the pitch. Beat that City.

It's a similar level of stupidity to the argument to claims that modern football with its upstarts flashing the cash, with its big wages, sponsorship deals, stadium naming rights and detachment from reality has somehow removed the soul from football. What actions remove the "soul" from your club? You know, that fabricated, nonsensical thing that a club doesn't actually have. If you do believe in such things as souls (I don't), then within a football club it is contained within each individual fan – until they leave, the soul remains.

Last night I watched a documentary on the Formula One racing driver Ayrton Senna. When Senna crashed his car and died at Imola in 1994, as the helicopter carried him away from the track, Jeremy Clarkson commented (in a rare moment of sensitivity) that it really illustrated Senna's soul departing. A nation mourned over a lost soul. It has never mourned over the name of a stadium or the wages of a football player.

Fans will always live in the past. Hope that your team's glorious European campaign of 25 years ago, or 15 years ago, or even 5 years ago is enough to attract the cream of world football, and recapture those glory days. But I would wager that footballers are more interested in the future, about creating their own history, and finishing their career and having something to show for it. Mascherano was right that you can't buy a history – because the history for every club in England, for every club in the world, is already there. And you can't buy what you already have.

The Season Begins – This Time I Mean It

So, to the 2011/12 Premier League season – you know, the thing this book is supposed to be about.

City started well. Sergio Aguero inspired City to a 4-0 win over a gritty Swansea, and a star was born, his 25-yard screamer a true statement of intent. Next came a 3-2 victory at Bolton, a nervy game lit up by a superb Gareth Barry goal. There were few nerves at White Hart Lane however as City destroyed Spurs 5-1, Edin Dzeko grabbing four goals, including a magnificent header and a superb late long-range goal. City saw off Wigan 3-0, and were coasting through the season.

Still, there was still plenty of time for City to hog the headlines off the pitch, as Garry Cook fell on his sword, after trying to cover up a misdirected email. Here's what I wrote at the time.

You could see it coming. Soon after the story broke, there was a certain inevitability about the whole thing, and last Friday Garry Cook finally succumbed to the media pressure over his email gaffe and resigned, to the delight of millions.

Cook has never been a popular man in the press, or with other clubs' fans. Seen as prone to gaffe after gaffe, keen on CEO-speak and too business-oriented, his departure will gain little sympathy. And on over a million pounds a year that's fair enough. The press had had it in for Cook for a while as he had lied to them about finding a successor to Mark Hughes – they obviously expected him to openly tell them they were looking for a new manager.

I am not sure when football club CEOs and board members became big news in football. The likes of David Dein and Peter Kenyon led the way by having a high profile, linked to the fact that many like them and David Gill at Manchester

United sat/sit within the FA and various European club committees.

And Cook was certainly high-profile, sometimes unwittingly. Overseeing one of the most talked about football stories of our time, he brought unprecedented growth in the club and its global profile, sometimes talking in the style of the marketing man that he is, a style that grated with many, who still see football clubs as some close-knit local community-type operation. Welcome to the 21st century. You might recoil at the thought that football is all about money and global profiles and marketing, but it has been that way for decades – that's not Cook's fault, and with the dawn of the Financial Fair Play regulations, Cook and the owners knew that City had to expand their profile and increase marketing in order to compete. He did his job, and he did it well, also helping to bring the best set of footballers to the club for a generation (possibly ever).

So like the game around him, Cook was about the money – some of his football ideas are to be dismissed, but he wasn't there at City for that. Every top club (and many others) has someone like Cook now – just because they don't say as much as Cook did publicly doesn't mean they're not doing the same things and thinking alike.

But Cook offered something else too that you won't see mentioned. Most people know only half the story.

As Oliver Kay of The Times astutely tweeted: *What I found endearing about Cook was that he cared about the fans. Very few do. And it's not just a £ thing. Do other rich clubs care?*

And he did care. There are endless stories of how Cook has helped City fans – sorting out complimentary tickets for games, spending endless hours chatting to fans and listening to their opinions, doing impromptu ground tours for visitors, and generally putting himself out when he didn't have to. Most CEOs wouldn't. He was the only guy that realised that an indoor ticket office in Manchester might be quite a good idea. Those that call him a buffoon tend not to have met him.

Introducing Uwe Rosler into the Manchester United Hall of Fame was a simple slip of the tongue. Unfortunate, and badly timed, but still just a slip of the tongue, and the pathetic overreaction by a minority of City fans was saddening. Defending Thaksin Shinawatra and saying he was a great guy to play golf with wasn't the best idea, but he could hardly not defend his owner when questioned. Let's be honest, most City fans defended Shinawatra until we realised he was doing more harm than good and that his excuses no longer stood up to analysis.

And for the record, Kaka did bottle it. So there. When the press are taking the side of Silvio Berlusconi, then you know there are agendas at play. Cook's comment was borne from frustration at the underhand methods Berlusconi used to scupper the deal, but he probably learnt that day to bite his lip a bit more in future.

As for the email saga, the whole thing stunk. Its sudden release 11 months after the event should set the alarm bells ringing. Onuoha's mother's assertion that seeing the email was worse than getting cancer is possibly the most ridiculous comment of all. Week-long media coverage sealed his fate, but he sealed it too by not coming clean at the time. The email itself was not a sackable offence – we have all made similar mistakes and said some nasty things in our time. It should also be seen in the wider context of the ongoing difficult contract negotiations and we do not know what else was said between the three parties – I am not excusing the mail, though I fail to see how it mocks cancer, but don't think he lost his job because of it. After all, this was a private email, where things are said that you wouldn't say in public – and that applies to everyone. His fatal error was trying to cover the whole thing up – once he did that he was doomed, and can have few complaints. If he had owned up at the time and apologized, it could have blown over. There were rumours that Cook was going anyway- that he would be moving back to America to be with his family who were already there. Manchester's two restaurants eventually wore them down too.

You see, throughout all the claims of the club's brashness, a lack of class and new levels of arrogance, the fans have never been looked after better. With a world-class team, world-class media production, fan interaction and low ticket prices (and even the best football kits ever) City fans have been spoilt, and Cook helped make it all happen. The club will hire someone else and move on (Inter Milan technical director Marco Branca is rumoured to be Mancini's choice), but be sure of one thing – he will be missed, and has left a wonderful legacy for the club. And if fans of other clubs didn't like him, well to be honest, who cares?

To be honest, it was getting tiresome having to endlessly defend my club for things that happened off the pitch. Since when did CEOs become such big news? Football is no longer just about what happens on the pitch – there is so much online space to be filled by journalists, that Balotelli's toilet habits or the colour of Cisse's hair is suddenly fair game for comment.

But then – disaster **ON** the pitch. Yes, City drew a game. Oh, the shame. A 2-goal lead was surrendered at Craven Cottage as City drew 2-2 with Fulham. By the reaction of a few City fans, I can only assume we were also relegated.

Before the draw with Fulham came another one, in City's Champion League debut at home to Napoli. It was an anti-climax for City as a skilful Napoli caused City all sorts of problems, City coming from behind to salvage a draw. It was the sign of things to come in a difficult campaign, and yet the most surprising thing for me was how little I cared. I wanted City to progress of cause, but our various failures didn't hit me that hard. Maybe in the future it will entice me more, but having been told for so many years that the Champions League was the pinnacle for any aspiring club, the reality was a bit of a damp squib. Or maybe I'm just a bad loser.

A tedious game against Birmingham in the Carling Cup was brightened by a rare appearance for Owen Hargreaves, but I wasn't there to see it. For the first time in years I had willingly missed a home match, my desire to go non-existent.

City somehow managed to beat Everton in their next game, but next up was a big game against Bayern Munich, where nothing of any interest happened. Ok, wishful thinking. It was the night City made the headlines for all the wrong reasons, and we all realised that Tevez was beyond redemption (for a good six months). But now, much later, did he have a slither of a valid point? Was he just refusing to warm up as he had done enough of that? Well if do he contradicted himself in the post-match interview, and he learnt, like others, not to cross Mancini.

The biggest shame is that for half an hour City bossed the game and should have had a penalty. But they faded away after failing to make their dominance count.

It was more media coverage that we did not need. When the Daily Mail will publish a discussion between Mancini and a player about a corner as a "major bust-up", the club has to be so squeaky clean all the time to prevent stirring in the media it beggars belief.

This is what I wrote at the time:

After the match, Mancini looked angry, shocked, almost dazed. He stated that Tevez will never play for the team again. He will speak to the owners in the coming days to decide on the next course of action, but it seems certain now that Tevez's days are numbered – in that second half he crossed a line, showing a disgusting lack of respect not only for his manager, the fans, but also his collegaues. And, as usual, he failed to get his story straight, and no doubt fed by his "advisor" and close friend Kia Joorabchian, changeded his story the following day, claiming he did not refuse to play, having said after the match he wasn't physically or mentally capable of playing. Only a fool would believe this pack of lies.

The incident seems to have proved a watershed with the fans too. Tevez has always, as he stated last night, continued to enjoy a good relationship with the fans despite his repeated transfer requests and troublesome behaviour – mainly due to the fact he always continued to give 100% on the pitch.

Not any more – after the match Twitter and football message boards were ablaze with comments from City fans stating in no uncertain terms what they thought of him – whilst he will still have support with a minority of supporters, he has lost the vital backing of the majority of fans. The best thing for everyone now is a stint in the reserves and a January move – on City's terms, for a fair market price. He has burnt his bridges in English football, but there will be plenty of takers abroad – Corinthians are still the favourites (if they have any money), or maybe even Paris St. Germain.

Still, the unrest in Munich didn't seem to unsettle the team. It was later claimed that Tevez's abdication to the golf courses of Argentina were the main cause for them seemingly throwing away the title, as he would have been invaluable in the tricky away games at the likes of Swansea or Stoke. Yet after Munich, the team went on a nine-match winning run, and Tevez was soon at the back of everyone's mind.

Blackburn, Aston Villa and Villareal were seen off, before the big one - the Manchester Derby, at Old Trafford. Throughout, City maintained a lead at the top of the table, but it was never more than five points (reduced to two throughout most of December).

In the lead up to any Manchester derby, the press of course like to feed little snippets out at very selective times. Sometimes it's tedious interviews from ex-players, or current ones. Sometimes it's hysteria whipped up about some trivial, non-event. Before the Old Trafford derby this season, there was a heart-breaking interview with our spurned ex-manager, Mark Hughes. It didn't go very well for him, as I commented at the time.

Hughes Interview Does Him No Favours

The key to great comedy is timing – something Mark Hughes seems to have mastered this week. The same goes for his agent, the lovable, cuddly Kia Joorabchian.

As misguided interviews go, this was up there with the best. On the day before the Manchester derby (and on the day itself), a couple of journalists released their exclusive interview with Mark Hughes, which discussed his time at Manchester City and Fulham. In it, he came across as an embittered, jealous loser, like the jilted lover that sits at home swigging vodka and listening to Alanis Morissette (though Sam Wallace over at the Independent was keen to state at the end of his article that Hughes was not bitter. No siree).

On pre-derby day, it was all about City.

"We went through a lot of pain," Hughes said. *"Other people have had the gain."*

Few City fans thought Hughes was fit to lead the team to the top. Many thought he should probably have been given until the end of the season, and City were criticised for the manner of his dismissal, searching for a replacement whilst he was still employed. Now without any bias whatsoever, I can honestly say that City did the right thing. You cannot dismiss a football manager without having a replacement lined up mid-season – it makes no sense whatsoever. It might seem cruel to the manager at the helm, but that's the life of a manager – he got a £3m pay-off to console himself with. What's more, it was two years ago – perhaps time to get over it? I'm not sure what pain he went through for other people's game, apart from not winning many games prior to his dismissal. Whatever, owners who have pumped a billion into a football club are probably entitled to install their own man. And he seems to be doing ok.

But the foolishness of his interview is less about whether he deserved the sack, but how he sees fit to comment on a manager far more successful than he will ever be, and all whilst out of employment, a blatant PR exercise to remind owners of his availability.

"I don't know the guy personally," said Hughes of Mancini, *"but looking at him from the outside, he comes across as autocratic. It's either his way or the highway. I'm not sure he indulges players, tries to get to know or understand them. I'm not sure he's that type of manager."*

A good rule generally when deciding whether to comment on someone you don't know, is to stay quiet.

"Managing like that in the modern age with modern footballers is more difficult. To be an absolute autocrat and not be flexible in terms of how it's going to be done and not understand your decisions can impact on players is difficult, because they do. If you manage like that, there are going to be clashes and the likelihood of having clashes with players is, on the law of averages, going to be more prevalent than managers who try to get the best out of players doing it the other way."

How bizarre to pass comment on how Mancini manages – Hughes must have the brain cells to realise how bitter it makes him look. If only Mancini could have managed more like Hughes and eclipsed his illustrious managerial record. Or perhaps become a bit more laid-back like that rather successful guy down the road – oh, hang on…

So what if there are clashes and fall-outs? Hughes seems to think players should be pampered – well I'm sorry, but that's drivel .They are paid obscene amounts of money (those at the top) and should do as the manager says. And tough luck if they don't like it. And there will always be fall-outs with managers and players – no style of management can avoid this.

"Carlos (Tevez) is strong-willed, certainly," he said. *"Yes, he wants to play and for a guy who has come through life the hard way he still has a genuine desire to want to play every week. I never saw him as volatile. I can't think of one incident where there were flashpoints, but I played a long time and I can handle things like that. You learn how to take the sting out of it. It would never have happened under my watch."*

Yep, suddenly Hughes is the master man-manager. Funny how he doesn't mention failing to handle Robinho, the biggest name at the club for much of the time, or his total failure to work with Elano, once making him wait outside his office for an hour like a naughty schoolboy. The reason he had little problem with Tevez was that it was the player's first season at City – and he tends to behave in his debut season.

Just how would he have avoided flashpoints? Well as mentioned earlier, by indulging the player. Well City tried that, and Tevez took advantage even more. It's a dangerous game to bow down to the whims of any player, and it tends not to go down too well with other players. Fancy that.

The best though was left to last.

*"Whether or not the group as a whole work as diligently and with the same mantra **Manchester United** have, I'd maybe suggest not. Every Manchester United player understands what United is about. The players understand it is a privilege to play for them. They show the club that deference. I'm not sure the group at City understand that yet."*

City fans are used to this oft-repeated rubbish that United players all play for the shirt, would play for free if necessary, and that City are just a bunch of over-paid mercenaries after the money at a club ridden with ill-discipline, and poor team morale. Well apart from the fact that if they were just playing for money it would be fine (it is their job after all), the evidence seems to suggest otherwise does it not? And if you are going to come out with such steaming piles of dog-poo, best not to do it the day before City beat United 6-1 at Old Trafford – it just makes you look even more stupid, and even more bitter.

By Sunday he had enraged Mohammed Al Fayed, and when the man that erects a statue of Michael Jackson outside his ground calls you strange, then you know you're in trouble.

"What a strange man Mark Hughes is," he said. *"Sacked by Manchester City, he was becoming a forgotten man when I rescued him to become manager of Fulham Football Club."*

"Even when results were bad, I did not put pressure on him. I gave him every support – financial, moral and personal. He fully negotiated a two-year extension to his contract. On the day he was due to sign, he walked out without the courtesy of a proper explanation. And now he insults the club, saying it lacks ambition, and the players who delivered an eighth position finish last season and a place in the Europa League."

In my opinion, he is an average manager who would be out of his depth at a top job. He surrounded himself at City with his friends (The Welsh mafia, or as many called them – The Tafia"), bought Jo and Santa Cruz for £35m, and lacked the imagination to take the club to a higher level. Rather than taking agent-led snide digs at a man he doesn't know, a man with a managerial record far to superior to his, perhaps he should concentrate on working out why he is out of work, and try to work on his own deficiencies. And when even journalists on Twitter are saying you sound bitter and twisted, then perhaps the problems lie closer to home.

In the lead-up to the season's first Manchester derby (spoiler alert: it went quite well), the monthly football periodical 4-4-2 were running a large feature on the rivalry between the two Manchester clubs. A twitter alert from a Mirror editor (and City supporter) to answer some questions resulted in the following submission from me. In the end they only quoted a few lines

(Andy Mitten co-edited it, after all), so here's what I had to say to the fellow blue who posed the questions:

Personal anecdotes of your lowest moment as a City fan (as you can imagine, I've got a few of these myself. Hearing United sing 'we'll never play you again' at the Lakey testmonial and actually believing it is one)

Where to start? Logically, relegation to the 3rd tier of English football should win but as it was my birthday and I knew it was coming I would argue there were worse moments. Even the nadirs in the season after as City sunk briefly to mid-table don't merit the accolade of "biggest low". What stands out for me came just before the relegation, a 1-0 home defeat to Bury, undoubtedly the worst game I have ever seen, or will ever see. Bury were just as bad, scoring with a deflected header that saw them clock up their first win in seventeen games. Legend has it that a City fan stormed onto the pitch mid-match and tore up his season ticket - the club posted the pieces back to him. Unlikely to be true, but that day I took a United fan to the match, for reasons that escape me. It's hard to recall if I was more embarrassed at City, or for inviting him along. It was the final, emphatic confirmation that the future was going to be very bleak indeed, and that relegation was a real prospect.

Personal anecdotes of when it clicked for you that City were about to become/had become the richest club in the world

I don't think there has been a precise moment when it clicked. It has been a surreal period in City's history, accompanied by the creeping realisation that things are never going to be the same. The day of the takeover itself, sealed with the signing of Robinho, was like a weird dream. An enjoyable weird dream, admittedly. There was no inkling that we were about to become so wealthy – I first heard about the takeover on the day it happened. There had been numerous vague rumours beforehand of Shinawatra looking to sell up, and it was clear he needed to, but I wasn't aware of the scale of what was about to happen. At the moment they announced on Sky Sports that Robinho was a Manchester City player was quite something.

If discussing the moment when I knew we had "arrived", perhaps more than anything it was the signing of Aguero recently – a player in his prime, wanted by some of the biggest clubs in the world - and he came to City. His signing has excited me more than anything, and right then I knew we were part of the football elite, a permanent fixture at the top table.

But more than anything, it was when Alex Ferguson started taking swipes at the club – proof, if proof were needed, that the noisy neighbours were one of the big boys now.

How the rivalry has changed for you in recent years. Are your United mates actually pleased for you? Do they fear City a bit now or do they think we'll cock it up again. Are they worried about United post-Ferguson?

It's hard to categorise how United fans have reacted as, with any set of supporters, you get a wide range of people, and United have three billion of them. Have no doubt though that they are worried. Fear? Maybe, to an extent. I find that strange to be honest, that after winning endless trophies for 20 years it should be City's emergence that would rile so many of them so much - but rile them it most definitely has. I think until recently, City were expected to cock up as always – after all, if anyone could waste a billion pounds, it would have to be us, and United fans had that thought to console themselves with. But once the FA Cup was won, it dawned on them that City are here to stay. The oil is not running out, and our owners have "massive" plans for the team and the whole community as a whole. It all depends I guess on what you mean by cocking it up – trophies will come, opinions will differ on whether it was a fair return on the investment.

For the hardcore United support, I think the competition is generally welcomed. There were seasons when City and United didn't play each other, which makes a mockery of a rivalry. So they wanted City to improve, but could never be happy at any success. For the part-time supporters and the Johnny-come-latelys that any successful club attracts, the reaction has been one more filled with spite. As for my dad, a United supporter, he seems pithily bemused by it all.

As for Ferguson, I don't detect too much anxiety from United fans, as his retirement does not appear to be imminent. City fans pray for the day he retires, as whoever follows him is on a hiding to nothing. No manager can match his achievements, and they will instantly decrease marginally as a force. United fans have realised that his achievements of recent years are as big as anything that went before because of what he has had to work with (relative to before), and it's that if anything that will cause the anxiety.

Has the vibe in the city itself changed as a result of our good fortune? Is Manchester an even more confident place than it used to be?

Manchester has always been a confident place - its inhabitants have considered themselves a cut above for quite a while now. But there is certainly a buzz about the place, once the smashed-up windows had been replaced. The national media have talked endlessly about the possibility of Manchester already being the football capital of England, and perhaps in the world, and that possibility has energised the city. I don't wear them myself, but the football shirts are on show everywhere – there is a pride once more in the shirt and those who play in it. And as a United-supporting friend told me, there is, deep within his soul, a tiny part of him that has a perverse pleasure at City's emergence because he loves his city and whatever you think of City's story, it has undoubtedly been good for Manchester.

Has the atmosphere at the derbies been heavier as a

result of City progessing. Coming out of the semi-final was horrendous....

The atmosphere has never been nice, at least not for a few decades. But anyone who went to the FA Cup semi-final will know that it is heavier now. There was a wave of nastiness that day on Wembley Way and it came mostly from one set of supporters. There has always been a minority looking for trouble, but the emergence of City as a force has intensified the hatred, helped of course by the increasing number of important derby games – no more are there just league games (some seasons) and the odd one-sided cup game. Now, the stakes are higher than ever, and if the two were ever to meet in a game as big as a Champions League final, it would be carnage. I don't think my heart could take it, to be honest.

When you go away, do you get the sense that City are as hated as United now? More hated even?

Undoubtedly City are hated more now, a hundred times more than before. This can only be a good thing. Before we were talked of as many peoples' second club – this is because we were a bit of a joke, failure seeping through every pore, and what's more, we knew our place. Kind sentiments came from sympathy.

No successful team is liked (even Barcelona are suffering a backlash now), so we have to accept that the more games we win, the more we will be detested. Few things lose you popularity more than breaking up the established order - they tend not to take it very well. As for the likes of Everton or Aston Villa fans, to name two random clubs, any hatred is more seeped in jealousy – City won the lottery three years ago, and we know it. Other fans must wonder "what if?"

Does the 'buying success' thing bother you? Have United bought their success to some extent? How did you feel about Chelsea when Abramovich took over? Did you the 'you've got no history' chant?

No, it has never bothered me because, despite what United, Liverpool or Arsenal fans may tell you, we are not the first team to splash the cash. United fans will argue that they earned the right to buy big by being successful. Liverpool have this amazing history (and City have none) that apparently bestows on them too the right to compete for the best players. Yet no other sport in the world rewards the successful in this way, and protects the status quo. In America they have draft systems precisely to combat this. The disbanded G14 and the threats of a breakaway European league couple with stock market flotations and Sky money have preserved the success of the same teams (more or less) for 20 years. There is no way to break this cartel without money – careful ownership, prudent buying and superb management may, if you are lucky, give you a brief moment in the sunshine (see Everton), but it won't last.

But more than anything I don't care because City have the best owners of my lifetime. I am watching the best football I have ever seen, for £460 a year, with the best ground, best facilities, best kit and best interaction with the club I have experienced. And who cares what other fans think? We are to a man (and woman) a bunch of prejudiced, blinkered, bitter hypocrites.

So what's not to like? Oh yeah, Garry Cook sent a nasty e-mail a year ago.

Do you think City could ever equal or topple United as a brand and as a globally supported club. How would you feel about that given all the jokes we've done for years about Japanese fans in jester hats and the Torquay Reds?

I doubt many City fans would want City to topple United as a brand. It is only Financial Fair Play rules that make trying to match them in these areas a necessity, so City can spend what they have earned. They certainly won't topple one of the world's biggest brands in the foreseeable future, no one will.

Only a spell in mid-table for United would dim their light, and I'd say that was rather unlikely. But the strides City have made in the past couple of years show that the gap has shrunk considerably, and will continue to do. City now have the 11th biggest revenue in Europe, and that's before they got into the Champions League.

As for the number if fans, I've seen United fans rave about the amazing turn outs for a training session in Malaysia for example, but I think I speak for many a City fans that I wouldn't lose any sleep if we had few fans in Asia – it is not a badge of honour for a football-supporting Mancunian. As long as I'm at the match, I couldn't care less what the attendance is, or who has more fans in Manchester.

Do you think Manchester will ever become a lifestyle destination for big football stars? Where do you see the clubs and the city being in 20 years?

You just can't get past the weather. It isn't terrible, but it isn't the Mediterranean, and a warm climate attracts (some) players. That said, it is of little use without a successful team too, so it is an issue when in competition with two particular Spanish teams more than anything. If Milan can attract top players then so can Manchester. If you'd been there you'd realise it has very little to offer that Manchester can't. And I'll wager Milan doesn't have a Pound Bakery.

Manchester has much to offer, and is surrounded by beautiful countryside. It is even working hard to open a third restaurant. Ian Brown once said Manchester had everything except a beach. Who am I to argue?

And as for the game itself – well I think you know all about that already. Here's a rare match report of sorts....

Manchester City's Corner: Fergie's Man United Stunned – What Are The Ramifications?

Even two days after that game, having read every match report available, it's hard to fathom a result like this, whatever the circumstances. Most City fans would have happily taken a draw away to the Champions. With five minutes, some feared a remarkable comeback or were bemoaning that victory might possibly only be by a single goal.

And yet, as always, the derby started with utter dread. The fear of conceding the early goal, of being thrashed. After all, Arsenal had conceded eight goals here just weeks before. There was little evidence in the early stages of the match of what was to come. United started as they usually do, coming out the blocks strongly and pressing the opposition. In the first ten minutes, City struggled to retain possession. But having ridden out the storm, City regained some balance as both teams failed to penetrate the opposition defence and test either keeper. With City's first clear opening came City's first goal, in the 22nd minute, and the nerves were somewhat settled.

And yet, the City of old, and the United of old too always hangs over the fixture. There were still lingering doubts in City minds, that feeling of dread, as late as the the 81st minute, when Darren Fletcher curled a beautiful shot past Joe Hart's despairing dive – if anyone could come back from such a seemingly hopeless position, it was United. In the end, there was no need for concern. Greater punishment came from City, first in the 90th minute, with Lescott turning a header from Gareth Barry into the path of Dzeko's knee. Dzeko then released Silva to finish through De Gea's legs. And there was a glorious flourish to come when Silva's vision and accuracy freed Dzeko to capitalise once more.

Manchester United 1 Manchester City 6 it read. A sight to behold forever.

It hardly seemed real. For United, too many players failed to perform. Evans is the obvious example, but he was far from alone. His defensive partner Rio Ferdinand had an atrocious game, and doubts must now exist over his future at United. The problem with Ferdinand is that his nonchalant style looks great when he is doing well, but equally bad when he isn't.

Patrice Evra, too, continued his two-year decline, and City got great joy down his side of the pitch. Out wide, Nani and Young failed to impose themselves on the match whilst Fletcher and Anderson were outmuscled in midfield, the situation made worse when Fletcher was moved to right-back. Welbeck was isolated while Rooney was forced deeper and deeper to help out his midfield. For City, there were no weak points. Mancini got his tactics spot on, and while Silva was the class act on the pitch, virtually every player gave an 8/10 performance or better.

By the end, no one could really comprehend such a score. The majority of City fans may never have seen anything like it, and it's unlikely they ever will again. The circumstances are merely an afterthought – the score itself will live in the memory forever. A ridiculous defeat for Chelsea later in the afternoon just added to the joy. Despite a delicate head, going into work the following day must have been easier than usual – a few United fans having taken the day off on short notice.

But what does the match signify? Sadly, probably not that much.

Roberto Mancini, grinning wildly during the closing minutes of the match, was more grounded than most, and summed it up best. *"It's not important 6-1. It's important that we beat a fantastic team. That is important,"* the Italian manager told Sky Sports News. *"It is important for our confidence because I don't think it's easy to come here. When you come here to play at Old Trafford it is an honour, because United are a strong team and you can have some problems."*

And amid all the elation, he is right. It was an amazing result, helped by a man-advantage for 45 minutes, and by City cruelly punishing a tiring United at the end. But it's a bit early to be declaring a decisive shift in the balance of power, despite the statistics.

And the statistics for the match are staggering. It was United's worst home defeat for more than half a century. It equalled the derby score-line of 1926, and it equalled the margin of United's biggest ever Premiership defeat. Already, City have scored more goals than they did in an entire season under Stuart Pearce – and a few other seasons before that too. In the last four minutes alone, there was a six-goal turnaround in the two teams' goal-difference. Could that be a vital factor come May? By full-time, the bookies had installed City as title favourites.

City now have the cushion of a 5-point lead at the top of the Premiership, and a goal difference 12 better than that of United. But it is early days and United are sure to bounce back. I wouldn't like to be an Everton supporter next weekend – United will be smarting, and Ferguson will demand retribution. United have suffered heavy defeats before – and usually gone on to win the league, such as after a 5-0 defeat to Newcastle followed by a 6-3 reverse to Southampton. They couldn't blame the colour of their shirts this time though.

City's tests will continue to come. If they are to capture the league, they must keep going all season, win when the inevitable run of bad form comes, and keep their cool at the business end of the season. With winnable games coming up in the league, it is vital they concentrate and continue to perform. City may have proved they have the better, and deeper squad – but Ferguson is the master at getting the most out of what he has – the bad news for United is that the constant attempts to portray City's players as mercenaries who have contributed to a poor team spirit seem wide of the mark. City players seem to be enjoying the challenge.

And what's more, the perceived negativity in big games may now have gone – Mancini has the squad he wanted (almost) and is happy to take any team on. There should be a lot more goals before the season ends, and more records broken.

All the while, Chelsea carry on quietly – the bad result of the weekend was a consequence of circumstances and even with 9-men, they were the better side against QPR. All the media hype of the power of Manchester football could play into their hands in the long run.

Either way, this was a result that will live in the memory of both sets of fans for many years to come, and go down as one of the greatest Premiership victories. It was a proud day to be a City fan, a magnificent declaration that City have the best manager for the job, and the clearest possible sign that City are now definitely a key player in the title race. The pre-match thoughts remain – this game was never going to decide or prove anything, but in the end it gave all City fans a memory to cherish forever. Any football fan has days when they wonder if life would be better if they had never fallen in love with the sport – but when it gives you days like Sunday, then you realise why you follow your team, and why you always will.

The derby result was strange for one particular reason. I remember as the 6th goal went in just laughing hysterically. I was past celebrating by that point, I just found the whole thing hilarious, ridiculous, stupidly bonkers. It just reminds me – however successful we may or may not be in the future, this season gave a couple of matches that may not be matched again.

After the derby, the winning run continued. Wolves were seen off twice, along with Villareal and QPR, in a nervy game at Loftus Road lit up by a superb strike from David Silva.

But whilst the win in London was met with relief, behind the scenes, the manner of the victory may have left scars that almost ruined City's season. For it was later rumoured that the ramshackle nature of City's performance that night startled Mancini so much (a man always seeking perfection, and whose Italian style demands defensive rigidity), he became much more cautious in future away games, with City's form suffering as a result. Only with the return of Tevez and the league seemingly lost did the team lose its inhibitions once more and regain the initiative.

Back Off The Pitch

The results were pretty good, but a couple of the English contingent had their own personal battles. For the in-form Micah Richards, his problems lay away from the Etihad stadium, and they were problems that did not go away right up to the Euros.

Micah Richard's England Woes

On Saturday evening, Micah Richards would have been a proud man. In the absence of the suspended Vincent Kompany, Richards was named captain for Manchester City's trip to QPR.

It was another plus point in what has so far been an excellent period in Richard's career. As the first-choice right back for the team five points clear at the top of the Premier League, he has been attracting all the plaudits after getting his career firmly back on track. Everything has been rosy in his particular garden – but he hadn't factored in Fabio Capello. On Sunday evening, Capello named his England squad for the upcoming friendlies against Spain and Sweden. It was a young squad, as understandably Capello looked at his options using two non-competitive matches. Despite all this, he thought Micah Richards didn't merit a place in the squad, for the team he first represented in 2006 aged only 18. The response was one of incredulity, and not just from City fans. Supporters of all clubs were mystified. As Annie Eaves (a Manchester United fan) of the Mirror tweeted: *When so many Manchester United fans are outraged that a City player isn't in the England squad then you know it's a strange decision.*
Joey Barton was incredulous. Darren Huckerby surprised. The cast of the Guardian podcast bemused.
Richards himself released a couple of tweets. The first simply

said: *ha ha ha ha ha ha ha ha <repeat to fade>*.
The second said: *Disappointment is an understatement!!*

His disappointment was understandable, as it is hard to know what more he has to do. He said in 2010: "It's definitely frustrating and every time the full squad's named and I'm not in there, I'm devastated, because I know with my ability that I think I should be. If you look at my England career, I've played 11 times and in all those games I think I've done reasonably well".
He said it again this week: "I know what I've got to do – keep working hard – and that's what I'll do."
But sadly for him, Capello simply doesn't rate him.

The rumour is that Capello has serious doubts still about Richards' defensive capabilities. If so it seems strange as Richards had improved immeasurably over the past year. If Capello really doesn't rate him defensively it simply is nonsensical to pick Glen Johnson instead, who offers nothing extra in defence, and isn't even a first team regular in a team 12 points behind city in the premier league(not that league position is everything, far from it). Kyle Walker has also been chosen for the squad- a perfectly acceptable decision as he is a player on the up, but I still don't personally think that at this precise moment he is better than Richards. Some have argued that the other two are superior going forward, yet the Premier League defender with the most assists do far this season is: yes, Micah Richards with four, on top of the other six goal-scoring opportunities he has created for team-mates. He creates more chances per minute on the pitch than any other England rival, and has a superior tackle success percentage than any of his rivals too.

Capello's big mantra has always been that he picks players on form, not reputation. His omission of Richards shows this to be rubbish. Richards may have fallen foul of circumstance, saving his worst performance for against QPR when Capello was in the crowd the day before the squad was named, but then the team as a whole was not at its best on Saturday night, not helped by Richards having to cover for Savic's difficult full premiership debut. If Capello is making judgements from one game he isn't worth a £60 annual salary, never mind £6million.

It seems his principles only apply to some. There's no question of an out-of-form John Terry losing his squad place, even with a racism investigation hanging over his head. Manchester United new boys Phil Jones and Chris Smalling were of course fast-tracked straight to England glory. To play Jones out of position in a qualifier rather than pick Richards was laughable.

Let's not claim Richards is perfect. A year ago I would have sold him for a set of training bibs and a multi-pack of Quavers. After being previously linked with a. £25m move down the road to United, he went off the boil, seemingly more interested in bulking up in the gym and DJ'ing. But he has come back strongly to recapture his form and concentrate on football. He has an excellent mentality, a professional attitude and is an extremely popular team member. He still needs to improve, especially on tracking back and concentration- he still has his lapses (and admitted so this week). But he is generally considered the best current English right back in the game, and for the England manager to not even pick him for two friendly games simply beggars belief. I despise the Capello-bashing that many newspapers have turned into our new national sport over the past couple of years. Not being picked for two friendlies is hardly the end of the works, and it helps City to keep their player fresh. But I feel for the player who must wonder what he has to do, and the actions of Capello defy explanation. All Richards can do is knuckle down and continue his good club form, count down the days until Capello is gone, and then wait for his international career to resume.

As it turned out, Capello's exit made no difference. And yet, a player who has made much less impact at City, and whose days may be numbered, found his way onto the pitch for England's friendly against Norway in May 2012. Here's what I wrote about him last autumn – I can't say my view has changed at all since then.

The Myth About Adam Johnson

It seems Mark Hughes was right after all. Roberto Mancini's autocratic style has claimed another victim, namely Adam Johnson. "Reports" emerged that he initially refused to get on the team coach after City's win over Wolves in the Carling Cup, due to criticism of him in Mancini's post-match interview.

Or maybe not. Many would have you believe that Johnson is being wasted at City, and that Mancini's criticisms of him are unfair. On both counts, they are wrong. As was Hughes, on many levels.

It's hard to claim that Johnson is wasted at City when he has improved as a player under Mancini's tutelage. He was playing in the Championship at Middlesbrough, and was hardly the first name on the team sheet there, sometimes kept out of the side by Stewart Downing. His England appearances have tended to come since his move to City. As Mancini said this week, he criticises him because he knows he can do better, and because he knows what he is capable of, and this is his way of trying to push him further. I'm not totally sure it's right to talk about players' deficiencies in public, because as we saw with his coach protest, players are generally precious souls, but in Mancini we trust, as after all he knows the player and the situation far better than I or anyone else does.

"I am happy he is upset," said Mancini this week. "I love Adam. It is like with the children in your family. If you love your children, then sometimes you should be hard with them and

Adam understands this. I say what I want because, if he were not a good player, then I wouldn't waste my time on him. But because he has everything, I don't want him stopping at this level. I want him up a level and then a level more."

The player who some claim is gathering splinters on the substitutes bench has appeared for City 54 times since he signed right at the end of January 2010. He made 43 appearances for City last season, and has featured 8 times this season so far. He is not the forgotten man that some would have you believe.

And if you want reasons for why he sometimes only appears from the bench, then the answer is there for all to see in the games he has started. Quite simply, he has not performed at the required level when in the starting eleven, with a tendency to disappear from games and have limited impact on proceedings.

From the bench, it is a different story, there being few players better at coming off the bench and putting the opposition to the sword. It seems he prospers against tiring legs, but if he wants to feature more he has to do it for 90 minutes, not 20. But it is something else that irks Mancini more.

With Johnson, the criticism from above has been that he is shirking his defensive duties, duties that are vital when you are a wide player that needs to support his full-back.

Mancini has said this week he was "disappointed he doesn't put everything on to the pitch". As he is right to do, Mancini expects it all from his players. He expects forward players to do their share of defending, in the same way he expects his full-backs to bomb forward.

In addition to all that, there have been concerns about his off-field activities and lifestyle – many a footballer has fallen in this trap, but Mancini is not the sort of manager to allow it, or to accept players that are not 100% focused on their football.

Nevertheless, his scoring record is beginning to look very healthy indeed. He scores quality goals, and often when they are most needed, making him a vital squad member. He is a wonderful wide player, the sort opposing defenders must hate to play against, with pace, close control, and as we have seen recently, a deadly shot.

A few years ago Johnson did an interview with Four Four Two magazine. The final question was:

In five years' time…

I would like to be playing regularly in the Premier League and challenging for a place in the England team. So far this season things have gone well so hopefully I won't be a million miles away by then.

And he isn't. The future is Johnson's to decide. If he wants to listen to his manager, the world is his oyster. At the age of 24, he has reached a crucial crossroads in his career. Knuckle down, and play for one of the best teams in Europe and at the highest level for club and country, or go on loan somewhere and gain more football at a lower level. The choice is his.

The Season Continues

Back on the pitch, and an excellent Newcastle side were beaten 3-1 at the Etihad before City's Champions League hopes evaporated in Naples. Napoli were excellent once more, in front of a near-hysterical home crowd, and qualification was out of City's hands as they deservedly lost 2-1.

But as was often the case with City, there was plenty more criticism to be had off the pitch. It was around this time that City announced their annual results – the response was predictable.

City's Record Losses In Context

You could sense the rage and indignation around the country as the news was announced. You could hear a collective tut and a million heads being shaken. Football had died (again). Manchester City had announced their annual financial results, and had posted the biggest losses in football history, a cool £195m for the 2010/11 financial year. They're Manchester City, they spend what they want.

Well not if UEFA have their way of course. And the inevitable response to the announcement was to reignite the debate over how they could possibly meet UEFA's new Financial Fair Play (FFP) rules.

Obscene losses? Perhaps. But less obscene than owners who wrack up debt, or owners who asset-strip clubs, or are there for personal gain alone. At least the money being spent is their own – but that's an argument that has already been done to death (but will have inevitably resurfaced over the past few days).

Rival fans might scoff at how the huge losses will cause City to fail to meet FFP rules, but it was these rules that bizarrely helped cause the losses in the first place. City's owners knew the day they took over what was on the horizon, and as Brian Marwood has stated in the past, the club embarked on an accelerated programme of expansion and purchases, "attempting to squeeze ten years' development into three".

Equally bizarrely, due to the ruling on "trends", the huge loss might actually benefit City. Why? Well the FFP rules are far from set in stone and far from black and white. The key to meeting the requirements is not simply to spend only what you earn, but to make movements towards that point (at least for the next few years). So for now City and other clubs have to be seen to be taking steps to narrow the gap between outlay and income, and City will undoubtedly do this – this year's figures are certain to be the worst by a long way, so the only way is down from now on (or up, depending on how you look at it). As long as the losses reduce each year, the club has little to worry about. Thus City have deliberately posted bad results – they have used last year's accounts to lump in all the deadwood and heavy purchasing before the rules get stricter – £35m of those losses are precisely for the writing off of deadwood, a one-off cost of players City know they won't get a good return back on. After all, if your wife told you to start behaving better as of next Sunday, you could be tempted to burn down the house on the Saturday (I could have used a better example to be honest). So whilst in theory a club can only lose €45m over the next three seasons, the fact is that UEFA will probably be quite liberal with that figure.

What's more, UEFA are highly unlikely to ban a "big" European club from the Champions League – in a sport ruled by money at the highest levels, it simply isn't in their interest. Ian Ladyman of the Daily Mail said as much on Friday, reporting that Michel Platini has softened his stance on punishing clubs, looking at fines rather than expulsions, a system that will not unduly worry City.

But as mentioned already, City will bridge the gap. Over the weekend came reports of a new kit deal at the end of the season which could be worth an extra £18m per year. City's huge stadium sponsorship and campus deal is not included in last year's figures, nor was any income from the Champions League, which City will expect every season now – even if they go out in the group stage, they will earn over £20m.

And whilst big-name signings will continue, they will become less common. What's more, as City now have a top-class squad, they will recoup more in player sales than of old, so will become more self-sufficient on that front.

FFP doesn't work in simple lines of income versus outlay anyway, and some losses can be discarded from calculations, such as for academy development, spend on infrastructure and the like. It's all linked to the insomnia-curing UEFA Club Licensing Handbook, especially its Annex XI.

For the purpose of the first two monitoring periods, i.e. monitoring periods assessed in the seasons 2013/14 and 2014/15, the following additional transitional factor is to be considered by the Club Financial Control Panel:
Players under contract before 1 June 2010
If a licensee reports an aggregate break-even deficit that exceeds the acceptable deviation and it fulfils both conditions described below then this would be taken into account in a favourable way.
i) It reports a positive trend in the annual break-even results (proving it has implemented a concrete strategy for future compliance); and
ii) It proves that the aggregate break-even deficit is only due to the annual break-even deficit of the reporting period ending in 2012 which in turn is due to contracts with players undertaken prior to 1 June 2010 (for the avoidance of doubt, all renegotiations on contracts undertaken after such date would not be taken into account). This means that a licensee that reports an aggregate break-even deficit that exceeds the acceptable deviation but that satisfies both conditions described under i) and ii) above should in principle not be sanctioned.

All perfectly clear I'm sure you agree – but the new point to mention in that cut and paste is the dismissal from calculation of player contracts agreed before 1ˢᵗ June 2010.

City's income will continue to rise and their costs will tail off, having probably reached their peak. Brian Marwood admits there is still plenty of work to be done to adhere to UEFA's rules, but I doubt anyone at the club will be having sleepless nights just yet. What they want soon though is the deadwood to be cleared for good (yes, that includes you Carlos), and for the academy to bear fruits within a couple of years to keep player purchases down. Until then, they just have to move in the right direction – on and off the pitch. Whatever the figures may suggest, it's a case of so far, so good. And however much whinging may emanate from non-City fans, the club hasn't yet broken any rules.

The slump caused by defeat in Napoli was partially continued with a tense 1-1 draw at Liverpool, before a scratch side beat Arsenal's scratch side 1-0 in the Carling Cup quarter final at the Emirates, Aguero scoring one of my favourite goals of the season. City would be playing Liverpool twice more in the semi-final.

Needless to say, there was more controversy and talking points hanging around City like a bad smell as Mario Balotelli found himself sent off once more in the Liverpool game. For once though, he was as much the victim as the culprit.

Mario Balotelli's Reputation Goes Before Him

The rant you're about to read is usually the classic sign of a paranoid football fan. After all, we all think that the world is against our team, the newspapers are biased, referees have got it in for us, we never get any credit. And as for opposing fans….

But still, despite all that, the ridiculous red card for Mario Balotelli last weekend against Liverpool suggests to me, that just sometimes, that paranoia is justified.

Referees will of course claim that they enter the pitch with no agendas, and make impartial decisions on each particular incident alone. This is clearly poppycock, because they are human beings, and human nature means they have pre-conceived ideas about certain players, and treat them differently as a consequence.

To suggest Wayne Rooney gets away with metaphorical murder on the football pitch is the same as suggesting that night follows day – you could offer many theories as to why some players are allowed to say what they want to a referee with impunity or get the benefit of the doubt over some hairy challenges, but they tend to be English, which is not to suggest a wave of xenophobia from referees in how they deal with players, but a certain leniency to many "stalwarts" of the game, a blind eye to many established Premier League players. Balotelli doesn't fit this description, he is the crazy youngster from far away who fires darts at youth players, almost burns down his house with fireworks, walks around with bundles of cash in his pocket, gets his friends to chat up women for him, receives 2000 parking tickets in a year and hangs around with the mafia. Well I read all this in the tabloids, so consider it to be 100% true.
When Graham Poll is appearing on Talksport decrying his hairstyle, it gives you a good insight into how match officials enter the field with agendas and preconceived ideas. Maybe Balotelli deserves it then. Hey, he doesn't smile enough for my liking, throw the book at him.

It's the reverse of commentators mentioning that Player X is "not that type of player" when he is sent off for a knee-high challenge. That player could throw kittens off bridges every night, he could have been sent off 40 times in his career, or he could have never fouled before in an illustrious 20-year career. It's all irrelevant – it was either a red card or it wasn't.

Balotelli's first yellow card was perfectly justified – an innocuous pull-back on an opposing player, but a text-book yellow card in the modern game. The second card was brandished on reputation alone, by a referee who has a knack of sending off opposition players at Anfield (Balotelli completing the hat-trick). Maybe I am being blinkered – after all I have read a few City fans and journalists write online that he led with his elbow, and thus it was a stupid challenge and he was asking for trouble.

But no, that simply isn't true. There was no elbow sticking out, only an extended arm which I presume he was using to try and protect the ball from the opposing player, as part of his whole body. Clumsy perhaps, but nothing more. His fate was sealed when the Liverpool player went down as if shot, clutching a head that hadn't come into contact with anything, whilst five or six of his team-mates crowded round the referee demanding a red card. Has football really become so averse to contact of any sort that Balotelli's attempt at a tackle for his second yellow card is now considered as fair game for punishment?

I'm not blinkered to Balotelli's discretions. His demeanour makes him a target on the field, though a professional referee should be capable of looking beyond this. I can see when he has done wrong – the red card at home to Dynamo Kiev last season was utterly justified and put paid to City's Europa League chances. A dismissal at West Brom though last season was even more ridiculous than the one at Anfield – we've been here before.

He's not the only one to be pre-judged on the field either, due to off-field controversies. Joey Barton is one that springs to mind (not that he is always innocent, as seen against Arsenal this season), a man whose reputation on the field is probably confused with what he has done off it. The truth is that there are plenty of Premiership players who have sinned on a football field far more than Barton, but attracted much less attention for it. Likewise, those footballers portrayed as professional wind-up merchants like Robbie Savage also carry a stigma onto the field with them. In 2008, the Daily Mail labelled Savage as the dirtiest player in Premier League history, based on numbers of yellow cards received (87), though apparently he has since been surpassed as the player with the most Premier League yellow cards by Lee Bowyer. And throughout his career, Savage was only sent off for his club side once. Was Savage really ome of the Premiership's worst ever miscreants on a football field?

Players are the victims of soft red cards all the time – it doesn't take much to get dismissed nowadays. If you agree Balotelli was hard done by, you'll also agree that he isn't the first, and he won't be the last. But lets hope that in the future, referees have the ability to see through his reputation, and judge him on the foul alone. Otherwise, discussing the disciplinary record of Mr Balotelli could become a depressingly common occurrence in the future.

Jingle Bells

Into December, and Norwich were easily seen off 5-1, Balotelli shouldering the ball into the net for one of the goals.

Next it was back to Europe, and an all-or-nothing game against Bayern Munich. City had to win, and hope that Napoli slipped up in Villareal. City did their bit, beating a weakened Bayern side 2-0, but Napoli won too, consigning City to Europa League football, despite having picked up 10 points in the group stage. And Villareal, who started the season in the Champions League, finished the season relegated from La Liga.

Barry Glendenning (remember him?) called City's failure to qualify as the biggest flop in football in 2011. Yes, that's right, picking up 10 points in 6 games in a hard group was worse than United's capitulation in a far easier group (I hadn't even heard of one of the teams in their group), or £50m and £35m strikers who couldn't score or any number of relegations. Nope, it was City's debut Champions League campaign.

With the chance of European glory gone, the focus turned back to domestic issues, and the week didn't get any better as City suffered their first league defeat of the season, losing 2-1 at Chelsea. Things didn't go well. After an early Balotelli goal a clear penalty wasn't given for a foul on Silva, then City fell away. Playing half an hour with 10 men didn't help, and a Lescott handball decided the game, as Frank Lampard converted the winning penalty.

Six days later though, and City secured a valuable win at home to Arsenal, 1-0. Stoke were then beaten comfortably, but the spell of troublesome away form was soon fully in flow when a determined West Brom team held City 0-0 on Boxing Day.

On New Year's Day, feeling rather fragile, I found myself on a train to Newcastle, and then a taxi to the Stadium of Light. City huffed and puffed, but couldn't get past a stern Sunderland defence, and to add salt into the wounds, a last-minute offside winner for Sunderland capped a miserable day. City's season was hitting a number of stumbling blocks.

There was no time to lick the collective wounds. The Premier League were perfectly happy to let City play again only two days later, as there was over 48 hours between the game, as City hosted Liverpool in the league in a night match. This was the second time City had been made to do this, a staggeringly stupid state of affairs. The first time it hadn't done City much harm, as they best Arsenal in the Carling Cup, and again City prospered, ending up 3-0 victors.

It was a good response to a difficult period in the season, and what's more, City had managed to go a few weeks without any major controversies or talking points. It wasn't to last.

The FA Cup 3rd round draw had produced one of the ties of the tournament. The two clubs going for the Premiership title were to meet at the Etihad Stadium, a draw both teams could probably have done without.

What happened next doesn't need elaboration. It's bizarre to lose at home to your greatest rivals and exit the cup and yet still feel pride in your team, but that's how I felt.

Nothing will ever change my mind about Vincent Kompany's tackle, as I have eyes, and can see what happened. There were some in the media that applauded the decision, using the two feet off the ground argument. But the fact is, it was the cleanest of tackles, with no malice, and not even Nani feigned injury. Rooney didn't even go up to the referee (at first) to complain. The other fact is, whatever the laws are, you will never, ever see another player get sent off in the same circumstances. City were robbed.

At half-time, three goals down, I feared that United were going to avenge the 6-1 drubbing at Old Trafford. No wonder I left the ground relieved therefore after a spirited 2nd half comeback that confirmed to me that City do now have a hold over United for the first time in decades. A league double only served to confirm this. That aside, it was sad to be out of the cup we held at the first hurdle, but United drawing Liverpool soon brought further relief.

Vincent Kompany's Unfortunate Red Card

When certain big decisions in football matches depend on the viewpoint of a single person, there are always going to be arguments, heated debates and disagreements. Michel Platini would have it no other way, arguing against the introduction of video technology as it would deprive fans of contentious decisions, injustices and other controversies that many want to see eradicated from the game, but that he (and others no doubt) think make the game what it is.

Not that video technology would have helped Vincent Kompany during the FA Cup match against Manchester United. Even after the event there is no consensus on whether the decision was harsh, though most people seem to think it was. I will be accused of bias naturally, but I thought it was ridiculously harsh. Seen live there was disharmony at the award of a free kick. When the red card came out there was disbelief, and that horrible feeling in the pit of your stomach when a football match that started with such high hopes disintegrates almost immediately into a living nightmare. When Ryan Giggs can "scissor" Aguero soon after and receive no caution at all, you are left to wonder what is going on.

But ignore the ignorant outpourings from footballers and commentators alike who seem to have no idea of the rules in the sport that pays them so handsomely. There is no written ruling on studs showing or raising your feet/leaving the ground, as most will be aware. There is no consideration to be made on how badly injured the footballer on the receiving end of the tackle may be, or how much contact was made. This is all irrelevant, up to a point. The referee has to decide of excessive force was used by the penalised player, and if an opposition player was put in danger. I considered the tackle to be clean, and I thought Kompany was in control throughout, though he did jump up first and went in harder than necessary (some will argue), but United were in danger of breaking on goal, so Kompany may have been more resolute in winning the ball fully. Anyway, others may disagree – the camera angle from behind shows a textbook challenge, the angle from closer to what Chris Foy will have seen makes it look worse than it probably was. Referees are told that both feet leaving the floor for a tackle is an invitation for a caution, as at this moment the player has in their opinion lost control, but if the other player is not hit then that is where it should end. We can only guess at what Foy think he saw.

The appeal by City was always doomed to failure – decisions like this are never overturned unless there is a clear error (nevertheless, about a quarter of appeals are successful), which judging by people's arguments on Twitter, this wasn't. As Mancini pointed out, Kompany has effectively missed five games because of one clean tackle, having been sent off early in the game, and having previously been dismissed for two bookable offences. Tough break. But the FA are not corrupt, biased, or part of some conspiracy theory that goes right to the top (god), they simply back their referees, which in theory is no bad thing. If there are a spate of poor red card bans being upheld, then we have to look at the source – are our referees good enough? But that's a debate that could go on for years.

Of course people will claim that the FA were happy to appeal against a three-match ban for Wayne Rooney when he kicked out at an opposition player whilst in an England shirt, and were delighted when the ban was reduced. But I think I'm right in saying their argument was not that the offence wasn't worthy of punishment, but that three match bans for internationals are excessive considering the scarcity of games. It is not a valid comparison.

"All we want is consistency!" is the cry heard after every debatable decision, as videos are posted online showing Rooney getting away with decapitating a fellow professional.

But that's the thing – you can't have consistency for decisions that are subjective, that are down to the interpretation of the incident by one man in black. Like judging what is a deliberate handball is or what is preventing a clear goal-scoring opportunity, many of the rules of the game contain grey areas open to interpretation. This isn't a failing of the rule-book, there really isn't any other way to do it. You can't have a clear rule for every single type of foul or discretion. We're stuck with inconsistency for ever, and that's just the way it is.

The fact that a footballer will now be banned for four games after a tackle that won the ball whilst barely touching another person seems ridiculous, and on the surface it is. But after the FA turned down appeals by Nenad Milijas and Joey Barton recently, this particular appeal was always doomed to failure. The fact that the majority of people who have seen the tackle think the red card was harsh is not enough to overturn it in the eyes of the FA, who are keen to back referee's decisions. Rather than claiming the world is against us and the FA has it in for our particular team, we will just have to admit that sometimes things don't go your way.

Winter Woes

Next it was the Carling Cup semi-final first leg at home. The overwhelming feeling I got coming away was that Mancini cared less for this competition than the Community Shield. Harsh perhaps, but City never really performed, and never looked likely to. Liverpool pressed, got an early goal, then retreated and took what they had. It was a depressing 90 minutes, because whilst it was hardly top of our priorities, it was a chance to go to Wembley again, and it will be a long time before I get bored of that. My bank manager was happy though. Still, it was a two-legged affair, so there was still plenty to play for.

City's emphasis switched back to the league, the holy grail of their season. The campaign was back no track with two wins, but it wasn't done in style. First came a 1-0 win at Wigan to help relieve the away-day blues, before the amazing and controversial 3-2 win against Spurs. Mario Balotelli was once more the main talking point, after a super-slo-mo replay viewed from 15 different angles on a constant loop on Sky Sports News got Balotelli the ban the media demanded after allegedly perhaps possibly hitting out at Scott Parker, causing irreversible damage to his 1950s haircut.

To defend Balotelli became increasingly difficult during the season, and to defend him for this particular action would inevitably lead to calls of bias – but the fact remains that you cannot be certain from the replays that he meant to harm Parker. And to make a general point, I am of the firm opinion that if you need to look at an incident in slow-motion and from various angles, then there cannot be a case to answer. If you have to look THAT hard, then how can a player be punished?! Play the incident at full speed and then decide – that's the speed it happened at, that's the speed the referee judged it at. Rant over.

Well not quite - here's what I wrote at the time:

Balotelli In The Headlines Once More

The news that Mario Balotelli had been charged with a stamp on Parker during Manchester City's dramatic win on Sunday was met with a dramatic sigh by me, but with little surprise.

I changed my mind twice on how bad the incident was, but settled on the opinion that he does impulsively kick out at Parker. I can't be sure of that, no one can, but the FA doesn't need proof to convict. The incident looks worse when slowed down and replayed from every conceivable angle until you find the outcome you want to see. Claims from other fans that he "stamped on Parker's head" as if we witnessed some vicious post-pub brawl are predictably biased and wide of the mark (he didn't actually touch his head, but intent is enough), as I doubt he knew he was kicking out at any head (not knowing where Parker was), but the movement doesn't look natural, and he will get a four-match ban.

Balotelli doesn't help himself. His first booking was ridiculous, one of many harsh bookings he receives whilst others around him foul with the regularity of an atomic clock, but he does invite trouble. Both with his demeanour, which referees should see past, but don't, and by occasionally leaving a leg in here or there. He has to mature to survive in the premiership, as referees will sadly be looking out for him now – in fact, they already are.

Conspiracy theories about the FA though are embarrassing. The FA is not out to get City. Alex Ferguson thinks the FA has it in for United too. Liverpool fans aren't too impressed with them at the moment, for obvious reasons. Sorry to disappoint, but there is not a top-secret cabal hidden away in the mountains of western Peru (named Bouncer55 after the leader's age and his late dog's name) deviously planning their next move to hinder Manchester City's resurgence. The FA chairman is not much of a City fan if that was the case.

Many City fans on Twitter who dared suggest that perhaps he deserved to be charged were labelled as traitors. Apparently you must as a fan remain blinkered at all times and support your player, irrelevant of what your eyes tell you. However, it's not surprising some City fans get slightly paranoid and defensive when Bale's equaliser is cheered by the whole press box at the Etihad Stadium. I'm sure their intentions were honourable, and they just wanted football to be the winner.

And as for claims of England hypocrisy regarding the fact they appealed the Rooney ban, people need to realise that the situations are not comparable. The FA did not appeal the ban because they thought Rooney to be innocent. They appealed because they felt that three-match bans are too harsh for international matches, due to their scarcity, an argument I happen to agree with. A kick at another player can see a player out of action for half a year. The FA never claimed that Rooney shouldn't be banned.

But nevertheless, the FA must stop being led by media campaigns, be it Wayne Rooney swearing into a camera or De Jong making a sliding tackle. The rules should be there for everyone, not just for players subject to witch hunts in the media. How many of you know about Peter Crouch's alleged eye gouge at the weekend? Well you wouldn't if you watched Sky Sports News on Monday. Basically this is the price that is paid by big clubs – bigger media coverage, more analysis, more scrutiny, everything ramped up to the max to satisfy Sky's hungry PR machine pumping out round-the-clock news. Even the Telegraph ran a story (anonymously of course) asking if Balotelli could be subject to police charges. As for Harry Redknapp, he was at his hypocritical best, keen to condemn a challenge he happened to have seen clearly, whilst not seeing his own player Huddlestone's appalling challenge last year. As always, we should not use managers as a moral compass.

But most galling of all is that on Sunday there were two hugely important, exciting games that shaped the title race and no one is talking about the football yet again, because of a two-day loop of a clash of players, and this happens week after week after week.

But there's little point in appealing the charge – the fact that the FA have brought it suggests they already assume guilt in the matter, and will back Howard Webb's assertion that if he had sent he incident he would have issued a red card.

And moaning about other players getting off with past indiscretions doesn't solve anything either.
Consistency! Every time a controversial incident happens, the word is wheeled out. But those players got away with it in the past for one reason. Essentially it's the rule of the referee seeing it that spared them, and it's that rule that, in my opinion, needs changing (but never will be). Let's stop backing their every decision, and accept they may not see things correctly, let's accept they are human beings and prone to mistakes, and allow retrospective punishments irrelevant of whether the match officials saw it or not at the time. How can we argue against players always getting a just punishment (though of course even with replays from 10 different angles we can rarely agree on many tackles). The system clearly doesn't work – if anything, Lescott's forearm smash was worse than Balotelli's indiscretion, yet he gets away with it whilst Balotelli sits at home for almost a month (not that I am convinced Lescott meant any harm either – something else for City fans to disagree over). The thing is that the rule gives referees a get-out clause over the ineffectiveness of their performance. There has to be real suspicion that referees are saying they haven't seen things when they have, so as to appear more competent. Players' futures are on the whim of what the referee says, and there have been many instances of referees claiming not to have seen an incident that replays show they were looking directly at.

But this is not an FA rule, so don't expect any change. As Graham Poll explained in March 2011 on the Daily Mail website (and he's never wrong), after Wayne Rooney's elbow on Wigan's James McCarthy was not punished further:

"....the referee dealt with the incident at the time and FIFA do not support the 're-refereeing' of incidents which referees act upon — whether rightly or wrongly. The statement issued indicates that referee Mark Clattenburg was happy with the action he took on the pitch. Without using video replays that does not surprise me.

Could the FA not have taken retrospective action anyway?

Only if no action was taken on the field. If that had been the case they would have sent a video clip to Clattenburg, who would have said what he would have done had he seen the incident. The statement would indicate that he would not have supported charging Rooney even if he had not seen what happened.

What changes should the FA make to stop this happening again?

This is where things get confusing as the FA say they are hamstrung by FIFA regulations and yet other countries (Australia and Holland, I believe) are acting retrospectively over diving. FIFA believes that referees must be supported, even when they make errors.

So we'll never have consistency. Players will get away with metaphorical murder, and they will sit out whole months after winning a tackle. City might have been on the wrong end of some questionable decisions this month, but most clubs do — especially if your club is big news. As always, blame FIFA.

Next it was back to Anfield for the Carling Cup. And yet again it was a tale of penalty woes for City with one of the most ridiculous decisions of the season as Micah Richards conceded a penalty after he blocked a shot and the ball rebounded onto his hand. Ultimately the game ended 2-2, and City were out. City's performances over the two legs did not merit victory, but the decisions went against them for sure.

It was a theme that was to continue on Merseyside. City crashed 1-0 to Everton, with another poor display not helped by yet again having clear penalty appeals turned down. Still, never mind, these things even out over the season.

Football Myth:

Decisions even out over the season

They don't. It's random. By pure chance your team's decisions may even out – but the odds suggest they won't, one way or the other. There's no magical being, no football god that looks over matches to make sure teams get justice after a wrong-doing. There's a devil in Sepp Blatter looking over us, but he doesn't like the one thing that could even things out, namely video technology.

It had been a tough January. City were struggling without the imposing presence of both Vincent Kompany, and Yaya Toure, who along with Kolo was away for the African Cup of Nations. But into February, and City continued their perfect home form with a 3-0 win over Fulham. This was followed up with a 1-0 win over Aston Villa, before an excellent double over Porto saw them progress in the Europa League. A 3-0 win against Blackburn and a 2-0 win over Bolton capped off a return to form.

There was soon a new elephant in the room though.

The Carlos Tevez Dilemma

It was the night before September 28th, and a creature was stirring. Manchester City were in the news again, for all the wrong reasons. A 2-0 defeat to Bayern Munich in the Champions League seemed almost like an irrelevance compared to the events that had happened just off the pitch, as Carlos Tevez, sick of being treated like a very wealthy poodle, refused to come on the pitch. Mancini was furious, his Latin temperament pushed to its limits, and when he declared Tevez would never play for the club again, few doubted him.

"If I have my way he will be out. He's finished with me. If we want to improve as a team Carlos can't play with us. With me, he is finished."

And yet, approaching five months down the line, here we are. Continual attempts to sell him have failed, and still employed by Manchester City, Tevez today returns to the training ground for <u>fitness</u> tests, defiant, adamant he has done no wrong, and no doubt considerably fatter.

I've little doubt that Mancini would be quite happy to get through the season without once calling on Tevez's services. But then again, if he can make a difference, he may well put differences to one side and look at the wider picture. However much any Ciy fan may hate him, Mancini probably feels the same, so if he is prepared to welcome him back then so be it, we trust in him. , If he was to make the difference, then my feelings for him are irrelevant – I would sell my soul for the League title. Some people seem to have struggled with the idea of him returning, basically equating it to having to welcome him back, forgive him, turn a blind eye to how he has treated the fans, and so on. We don't have to do any of those things – he can come back and help us to the title without being welcomed, without us forgiving him, without a heartfelt apology – the important thing is that the club does whatever is best for the club – that's all that matters, and our individual feelings on the matter are neither here nor there. No one is glad to see him, there's no high-fives from a minority of City fans, just an acceptance that he's back and the club might as well utilise this fact rather than acting out of spite and sulking.

Of course all this could be nothing more than both sides covering their backs legally – if City want to get some money back on Tevez, they have to be shown to be prepared to play him again, to show they are not to blame for all this, should it end up in a court room – and the same goes for Tevez and his representatives. If he's not in the Europa League squad, I really can't see him getting much time on the pitch. Famous last words eh?

But it seems many of the City fans want an apology – they demand it. Without that apology, there can be no return for Tevez, until he accepts that what he has done was wrong. Say sorry and it seems many will accept his return, because that one word will change everything. That one word in a scripted statement that Tevez's pen will have gone nowhere near. Personally, I couldn't care less if he apologises. It changes nothing, won't be sincere, won't change the past, and won't help improve results, so is pointless.

It seems Mancini demands this apology too though.

"Ten days after what happened in Munich, I invited him to come to my place to talk. I told him that, if he apologised to me, to the club, to the team, he could come back into the squad. I would have forgiven him. But he replied that he didn't have to apologise to anyone," said Mancini on December 5th. And Mancini made it clear on Sunday, following a 1-0 win at Aston Villa that he was still seeking an apology from Tevez.

But ignore the hand-picked comments from Sky Sports News and the tabloids, all happy to ignore the context in a 50-minute article. Ignore the fabricated Daily Mail article about City fans burning his effigy. The basic facts are that Carlos Tevez acted like an idiot, fell out with his manager, but the club couldn't sell him. Now he's back on big money as before, and both sides have to deal with this the best they can. He may be detestable, he may have acted terribly, but players are employed not to win popularity contests but football matches, and he has been punished financially for his indiscretions.

And maybe he will apologise anyway. To aid the situation, it is believed Tevez will drop his appeal to the Premier League against a six-week club fine, totalling around £1.2million. And his lovable representative Kia Joorabchian said the other day: "*This is between Mancini and Carlos. I think one of the things that is important is that Mancini and Carlos resolve their issue, and I think they have pretty much resolved their issue, behind closed doors and I think what is important is that the football takes over.*"

And the striker revealed he was ready to apologise if the club deemed it necessary.

"*I do not think I was wrong, but if they (the club) think so I apologise. I am ready to return, to win and do the best for the club's shirt,*" he added.

As for his team-mates, and fears that he will unsettle a title-leading squad, it is not vital that players don't have to get on with each other – Teddy Sheringham and Andy Cole at Manchester United famously detested each other, though it didn't seem to do them any harm. Having said that, I've seen no evidence that he will come back to a bad reception from the City players. In fact, the opposite seems the case, though the current wave of media-trained players will always say the right thing.

"*He is a good player and we'd welcome him back,*" said James Milner "*He showed how good he was last year (scoring 24 goals). He was fantastic for us. What's gone on or what's happening is nothing really to do with the players, but if it gets sorted out, then great. It means it's another top player for us to add to the ranks.*" And as I type, Joleon Lescott has tweeted how he is happy to have Carlos and the Toure brothers back to help City reach their goal.

Mancini is the main concern of course, but Tevez can only be involved in 14 games this season, in my opinion is unlikely to feature more than the odd substitute appearance away from home, and by apologising to all and sundry (without meaning it) won't really make any difference. City pay him over £200,000 a week – if he can help the club in any way, let him start earning it. Let him off the leash for one last time, and everyone can come out this affair happy. It's got to the point where neither side has much choice.

Time For A Rant

I was getting increasingly annoyed again (for a change). It can happen with fellow football fans. The world was turning on Manchester City again, and their "hapless" manager, because they might not win the league that few predicted they would do anyway. So there was only one thing left to do: stick up for him, and his players.

The criticism will be immense. There will be the inevitable claims of failure. Twitter will fall over with taunts from rival fans, mostly Arsenal ones mocking Samir Nasri for deciding to leave their club. The knives will be out, and sharpened, then thrust forward. The message will be clear: that with a "warchest" of £500m/£600m/£1 billion (delete according to which journalist you follow), with a squad clearly superior to all others, with a lead in the league table for the past five months, and at a time when many of its rivals are in disarray/crisis/process of rebuilding (delete according to…..), that Manchester City surely HAD to win the title this season. Which of course they may still do, and are still the bookmakers' favourites to do so.

But Sunday saw a shift in the title race, because Manchester United had come through their difficult spell of games, the spell during which most expected to see City extend their lead to at least six points, and yet they are still only two points behind. Now United have a run of very winnable games that could see them go into the powder keg of the Manchester Derby on 30th April as league leaders. And as their players tell us on a daily basis, they have the experience of a title-push, whilst City haven't, so City will probably bottle it.
Many blues are jittery now. The odd few, fuelled by decades of false dawns and base comedy, have almost thrown in the towel. All a bit over the top of course, considering City are still top of the league, but that's football fans for you.

But what more could Mancini really have done? Of course there are those simpletons in the media who would have you believe that such an expensively assembled squad should win every single game, steamroll every opponent, break every football record in sight. Because that's how football works eh?

Needless to say, much of the assembled talent isn't actually on the pitch. Emmanuel Adebayor is over at White Hart Lane. Carlos Tevez has spent more time in Argentina than England, Kolo Toure had plenty of time to think about his waistline, and with his brother left our shores for Africa for over a month (not that any manager can complain, they know the rules, though having one next year as well seems a bit harsh), and as for Roque Santa Cruz, well frankly who cares?

But misbehaving mercenaries apart (not my words), City have only failed to win six league games all season. If they finish second, it may well be the highest points total in Premiership history not to win the title. As it stands, they have scored more goals than any other team, and conceded fewer (by a long way). They've won 19 home league games on the row. They've beaten Newcastle's Premiership record by winning their first 14 home games of the season. Their goal difference is plus 50, ten better than United's. It's 31 better than Tottenham's, who in 3rd place also have the 3rd best goal difference in the league, but are 13 points behind City. And City are 20 points clear of Chelsea, the biggest spenders of the past year, the other "mega-bucks" side. City were the first team to reach 60 points this season. And the first to reach 50, 40, 30 and 20. Joe Hart has kept more clean sheets than any other keeper. Some of the individual player stats compare favourably not only in the Premier League but across all the top leagues in Europe. Basically what I am saying is – they've done pretty well. It's just that another team might do even better. As Roberto might say: is football.

Naturally it's the manager that takes the bullet for under-performance – Andre Villas-Boas is proof of that, at a club where his senior players acted like spoilt children, went running to the press, and undermined his efforts at every turn, whilst failing to show enough effort themselves when on the pitch. Which is to say that players are the ultimate deliverers of success or failure. It's about time the buck stopped with them every now and then. The players are there for City, the system in place, the lead at the top still similar to what it has been for many a month, so it is time for the players to carry the team over the finishing line just as much as Mancini needs to.

So if United go on to win the league, then perhaps it would be wise not to chastise Mancini and talk of chasing Mourinho to replace him, meaning another period of rebuilding, new ideas, and discarded players, but to doff our metaphorical caps and accept that Ferguson will have pulled off the greatest achievement of his career.

City have failed to pull away because of key away games. Defeat to Everton showed that old habits die hard. Defeat at Sunderland was an exercise in utter frustration against a massed defence – and it is City's struggles to break down two lines of defence on occasion that may cost them dear. Though of course United continuing to win hasn't helped. Either way, they've maintained their lead for months, and now face a trust test of their mettle. If they can maintain their lead from now on, then they will have truly earned it. If not, forget the post-mortems and recriminations, and accept that it wasn't to be. And pray that Ferguson retires as soon as possible.

Back in Europe though City crashed 1-0 in Sporting Lisbon. More damaging though was the same score line in Swansea that made me think for the first time that the title campaign may be slipping away. City looked jaded, as Swansea also missed a penalty. Their away form was beginning to cost them dear. City had lost the lead at the top of the table. City were soon out of Europe too, on away goals, despite a stirring comeback, but you wondered how much Mancini or the players cared. All thoughts were now on capturing one trophy.

Football Myth:

Away goals count double. They really don't. Ever.

On 21st March came a crunch match at home to Chelsea. City played well, but when Chelsea took a fluke lead in the second half, City's season was unravelling. But like they did on many other occasions, City dig deep and in the end Nasri fired home a late winner after a beautiful move.

The optimism didn't last long though. What followed was a dour 1-1 at Stoke City, the game that featured Peter Crouch's wonder volley (preceded by a foul on Gareth Barry, not that any report mentioned it). and then the 3-3 draw at home to Sunderland, City's 100% home record in the league coming to an end on a day when the defence was all at sea. Now the title had pretty much drifted away. The week after, it was surely all over. A woeful performance at Arsenal saw a 1-0 defeat, and Manchester United stretch their lead at the top of the table to eight points, with only 6 games to go. It was surely over, after a capitulation that the Guardian's Jacob Streinberg rather stupidly called the greatest title capitulation in Premiership history. United had got one over us again. Fred Done paid out on United winning the title. Champ20ns t-shirts were on sale. Mancini's job was on the line, which rather pathetically was welcomed by a minority of City fans. Speculation abounded if City's owners would fire Mancini, or whether Mourinho would take his place.

YES SIR

There was only one explanation for City's capitulation of course. The "wizard" had done it again. As City stumbled through the late winter, it was only a matter of time before "it" was wheeled out. IT was of course Alex Ferguson's mind games.

The Myth Of Alex Ferguson's Mind Games

I once watched an Alex Ferguson press conference on Sky Sports News. He commented on the danger of **Wigan** being cast away at the bottom of the table. He said that once a team was cast away at the bottom of the table, it was hard to recover, because being cast away historically meant relegation. The next day, for reasons that escaped me at the time, I went to live on a desert island for six months, wearing only a loincloth and surviving on a diet of coconut milk and papaya leaves. Only when I returned did I realise what had happened. Damn you Ferguson.

Look at why Roberto Mancini has become addicted to eating fruit pastilles on the City bench. Here's a spoof extract from what Ferguson's programme notes may look like ahead of the Old Trafford derby:

*'The match will be an intriguing contest between two title-chasing sides and Roberto will be keen to get one over our team, especially due to his love of fruit pastilles. Both teams will be looking to attack. Fruit pastilles. I'm pleased that **Jonny Evans** has had a good week in training, and we'll be looking for him to put in a performance today. Eat more fruit pastilles Mancini. Eat them until your teeth drop out. Ha ha ha ha!!!! PASTILLES.'*

One of the biggest myths of the past decade has been the effects of Alex Ferguson's legendary mind games, games that leave opposition managers broken men, nervous wrecks, that leaves players as pale shadows of their former shells. A little dig here, a pithy response there, and entire league campaigns fall to pieces. And the press are to blame for this, loving to "big-up" his every utterance into some sort of meticulously chiselled campaign to give his team the edge. It's just a shame (for them) that the facts don't seem to back up this viewpoint.

There are two shining examples of rival managers somewhat losing the plot during a title-chasing campaign against United. First of course was Kevin Keegan, who would have loved it, loved it, if **Newcastle** could have won the **Premiership**. A mental breakdown caused by Ferguson and his team? Not really – their form had been faltering for months, their defence faltering even more. They lost the league without any help from across the Pennines. As Garry Cook might have said, they bottled it, whilst United did what they always do and continued to notch up the points. Watching your team squander a 12-point lead in their quest for a first ever title is I imagine quite stressful, and eventually it got too much for Keegan, for whom managing England was also too mentally draining. Keegan's rant came after a Newcastle victory, but it came at a time when **Manchester United** had already overturned the previous deficit and built a three-point lead in the title race. For Newcastle, the damage had already been done.

Then of course there was the Rafa Benitez press conference, where he regaled us all with a certain number of facts. Again, was this Rafa feeling the pressure, him cracking up after a war of words with Ferguson? Well maybe he was feeling the pressure, most would, but it certainly didn't affect the team. Liverpool's form was better after Rafa's rant, and they managed to even stagger to a 4-1 win at Old Trafford – not bad for a side that had been destroyed by Ferguson's mind games.

It's a similar story for **Manchester City** this season. If United go on to win the league, which now seems the more likely outcome, it will be due to a couple of factors that have nothing whatsoever to do with anything Alex Ferguson might have said – namely United's possible record points total, and City's struggles away from home since last year. A sly comment in a press conference hasn't made City's strikers freeze in front of goal in Swansea or **Stoke** or **West Brom**. A well-timed barb didn't cause City to get a player sent off at Stamford Bridge or fail to mark a Swansea player a couple of weeks ago. The myth of his mind games can be filed with the other myth doing the rounds in the press at the moment, namely that City have squandered a 7-point lead in the title race (a lead they have never had except when having played a game extra).

It also ignores the fact that despite Ferguson coming out on top much of the time, be it a title chase, or a cup competition, he doesn't always, and no doubt when Mourinho beat him to the title or Guardiola's Barcelona showed their class at Wembley, he had plenty to say about football as well. Do mind-games not count when he loses? Or maybe they don't translate well into Spanish.

The latest "war of words" was started by a **Patrick Vieira** comment, and doesn't seem to have anything to do with Roberto Mancini. Vieira's barb (it wasn't even that to be fair) seems to have worked, garnering an angry response from Ferguson (not that I could care less about the whole affair), and yet many in the press, especially his little lapdog Bob Cass at the Daily Mail, have reported this as Ferguson once more triumphing in the mind games, or as one Mirror journalist put it, "putting Mancini in his place". Strange that, because as Rory Smith at the Times rather pertinently pointed out, if the roles had been reversed and Mancini had responded to a David Gill comment, the papers would be once more trumpeting it as a victory for Ferguson, goading City into a response. But as I said earlier, I really couldn't care less.

And I doubt managers or players do either. No manager worth his salt would be distracted by anything another manager says. Few players would care in the slightest, especially foreign players who are unlikely to have even heard what he has said. The pressure comes on the pitch, not off it. The top players, the players conditioned to excel at the top, will perform when needed, others will falter.

Which is a shame really, as Ferguson says he has plenty more ammunition, which doesn't bode well for City. Let's just hope they can shake off the psychological damage in order to put up some sort of title challenge next season. Now, where are those wine gums?

But in my pessimistic mind at least, it did look like the league was slipping away. Various reasons had been given for why City were limping towards the finishing line, so I decided to list them.

The Factors In City's Faltering Grasp On The Title

As it seems increasingly likely that the Premier League title race is fizzling out to a predictable conclusion, the inevitable recriminations will begin as to how it all went wrong for **Manchester City**. There'll be plenty of clichéd nonsense in there – the mind games of Alex Ferguson, City "bottling it", the bad team morale that saw brawls over the morning porridge on a daily basis.

The title race isn't over just yet of course, but City face a tough task to turn things around, and it is now out of their hands. So what were the reasons for City falling away? Here's a list of suggestions in a vaguely decreasing order of importance:

The Away Form

This alone could be used as explaining how City have lost their lead in the league. Since a nervy 3-2 win at **QPR** many,many months ago, City have been utterly underwhelming away from home. Even wins at **Wigan** and **Aston Villa** were nothing more than workmanlike, but what characterises their away form over the past five months is how chances have dried up. City haven't scored many, and haven't looked like doing. Tied to this seems to be a lack of Plan B – pretty passing with a reluctance to shoot is reminiscent of

Arsenal during the last few years, and opposition teams seem to have sussed City out. The team needs more width and pace away from home, and to return to the days of full backs bombing forward and putting in plenty of crosses.

Alex Ferguson

Or you could just use this reason instead. If he wasn't United manager, City would have probably sealed the title by now. But no one can squeeze more out of a squad than this man, helped by being in charge for a quarter of a century, and being rather good at his job – extra reason for Mancini to be given more time to try and build his own little "empire". And this ties into experience. That's the experience of the managers – many United players have no experience of title campaigns, but they are led by a manager who must be getting almost tired of them by now. The constant drivel in the media about mind games and the utterances of players and ex-players every day about experience has been tedious beyond belief, but experience must play a factor (though everyone has to win a title for the first time), and Ferguson collects trophies like I collect take-away menus.

Roberto Mancini

The fact is that he has made mistakes, which is to be expected in someone trying to win the **Premiership** for the first time. The early season form away from home may have frittered away because Mancini couldn't resist returning to his cautious ways when the heat was turned up. Then there's the strict style of management and the freezing out of players. I've been all for it personally, but others will point at his approach to certain players as being counter-productive. Mancini has appeared ice-cool over the past two years, but he has the look of a troubled man recently, and has become more surly with it. On this week's Guardian Football Weekly **podcast**, special guest Pedro Pinto commented that all his colleagues in Italy mentioned how Mancini struggles to motivate players, to elevate them. Having said that, he also said one of the reasons that City had let the league lead slip was that City's defence wasn't up to scratch (the meanest defence in the

Premier League), so he clearly isn't as clever as he seems to think.

Manchester United's Form

If I had a penny for every City fan that had said what United do is irrelevant, it's "in our hands", then I wouldn't be writing this blog, I'd be relaxing on a beach in Antigua. Of course it matters, it's how league tables work. If United had hit a rough patch, or performed as some feared they might with a less than vintage squad, City could be cruising to a league title, and probably playing a more relaxed style of football too. After all, their much-criticised away form is still probably going to be their best in premiership history (not saying much, admittedly), their home form could be one of the greatest ever, and they have the tightest defence and had outscored everyone until recently. But United haven't let up, so the bar has been raised this season, and it has needed a huge points total to take the title. Last season United won five away games and won the league at a canter. City have so far won seven, and have Top Three form for 2012.

David Silva's ankle

David Silva's form has fallen away, less surprising when you consider he is carrying an injury, and has been for months. But tied to the faults of Mancini has come the decision to play him almost relentlessly. Hindsight is a wonderful thing, but perhaps City would have gained more in resting him for a month or so.

Fatigue

Can this be mentioned? Are these poor souls allowed to get tired? Well of course they are, it doesn't matter if they are paid ten or a hundred thousand pounds a week, they are still human beings. That said, this is not a major factor. City's recent fall in form has come with little else to distract them. They may have suffered from fatigue in a disappointing January period, but it certainly can't be blamed for the lethargic showing against Sunderland, or the previous draw to Stoke. But it is worth mentioning that perhaps one of Alex Ferguson's greatest strengths is running a team that rarely appears tired. Their run of injuries may now (perversely) be benefitting them, as they continued to pick up points throughout and now have players soming back that have not been worn down by a full season.

The African Cup of Nations
If this is a factor, it doesn't bode well for City, as there's one next season too. Not an excuse, as we all know the rules, and all teams suffer to some extent usually, but it seems to have affected City more than most. They had a difficult January, when it bacame crystal clear just how integral Yaya Toure was to City's team, and what's more the returnung Toures have had no break, and Yaya Toure hasn't hit the heights since. In all, United dealt with absences better – losses of Kompany, Yaya Toure and Balotelli affected performances. Drug bans, suspensions, international competitions and players on strike – just your average season at City, and all a distraction from the football.

Carlos Tevez
Hard to pin a title failure on him as Sergio Aguero was essentially a replacement anyway, and every fan would rather he had been sold in the summer or January, but he could have made the difference in the succession of away games where City struggled to score.

The Busby Babes Looking Down On United
Not my words, but Martin Tyler's. What chance did City have?

Speaking of being annoyed, there's nothing that can annoy more than a moralistic Arsenal fan. Arsenal fans haven't taken City's rise very well. In fact, they've taken it worse than United fans. They simply cannot comprehend that their "doing things the right way" could possibly not be the template for everyone else. Never mind the lack of success or the ludicrous fleecing of the fans through high ticket prices, no, they do it the right way, and no player in their right mind would want to leave them, as it would be a backwards step. Being joked at as City's "feeder club" hasn't helped. Thus, they could not comprehend Samir Nasri moving to City for footballing reasons. It had to be about the money didn't it?

I wrote a blog in March on the subject.

Time For Arsenal Fans To Move On

For some it seemed more important than the match. Samir Nasri, Arsenal fans' arch-nemesis, was returning to the Emirates for the first time (in the league) since his contentious move to Manchester City last summer.

Ever since that move, he has been the devil incarnate. He only moved for the money, you see? Arsenal fans cannot contemplate a player leaving their team to try and better themselves – no, he was just a mercenary. What's more, after leaving, he said some nasty things too. Footballers eh? They just don't care. They don't get "it".

Arsenal fans will claim that they worshipped the player and he paid them back by leaving. They will argue that the club made him the player he was, and look at how he repaid them. Of course others will contradict these views by claiming he was only good for half a season anyway (so surely they'd be glad at getting a good price for him?), and have spent the past year laughing at every match spent on the bench or under-par performance (again, he has played a large amount of matches, but let's not allow facts to cloud a concerted campaign). Besides, as the odious Piers Morgan was keen to point out at the weekend, overjoyed at Arsenal moving towards ten points of City, Arteta is a better player than Nasri will ever be anyway. Which again begs the question – why are you bothered about him leaving anyway? But as Nasri was today announced as City's March Player Of The Month, perhaps we shouldn't believe everything we read.

Arsenal didn't "make" Nasri. He was an established player at Marseille, and a French international. They didn't buy him as an act of charity, to help him, they did it to improve their side, which he did, then got a very healthy profit when he moved on. Was he a mercenary for leaving Marseille, or do morals only count when it's your team being let down?

The fact is, Nasri wanted to move on. If not to City, then somewhere else. It's a job, and he wanted out, as he didn't see a successful future for the club. He might be proved wrong, but as many Arsenal fans wanted Arsene Wenger out only a few months ago, you can see where he was coming from. It's no different to Piers Morgan fleeing disgraced across the Atlantic for more cash (the cheerleader for the Wenger Out movement and chief bully of Nasri on Twitter), and I would leave my civil service job before you could say gold-plated pension if a better offer came along.

Carlos Tevez wanted to leave Manchester City too. He still does I would imagine. Fine. He is allowed to have this view, without becoming Satan himself in human form. Changing his story more often than a Murdoch at the Leveson enquiry and refusing to play are less agreeable of course, but I'd never spend a year of my life crying behind a keyboard because a player wanted to leave, or deluding myself that he'll win fewer trophies at his new club. It might be a disaster for him, it might be the best thing he ever does.

The other accusation is that Nasri made some nasty comments after leaving north London. Apart from the obligatory "my new club is great and the fans are passionate" line, saying the Arsenal crowd was quiet probably wasn't the best idea, but then as many Arsenal fans have made the same point, then what's the problem? Other quotes attributed to him seem to be fabricated, not appearing in the original French interview (as pointed out by the Daily Mirror journalist Annie Eaves, who checked), so as usual a footballer is damned by more lies spread around the internet.

But let's cut to the chase. What this really boils down to though is Arsenal fans' hatred of City's oil-funded wealth, the wealth that has put over £75m into their coffers. Better a system of income off fans through high ticket prices and the riches of Champions League qualification. The fans' hatred of City has been channelled into one player, and he is taking the brunt.

Still, we love to boo players. Even Gael Clichy, who left the Emirates on good terms, was booed on Sunday, as was Jose Enrique recently when he returned to St James' Park (or whatever it's called). Players just aren't allowed to leave a club, unless the manager demands it or the fans are happy with it. Otherwise, the player is a mercenary and a Judas.

The playground heckling has reached the stage of Samir Nasri and Piers Morgan betting £10,000 on which side picks up another trophy first. It's all rather pathetic from grown men – Nasri made a move that he thought would benefit his career. He may be proved wrong (he wouldn't be the first or the last), but that was his decision. It's about time everyone moved on before embarrassing themselves any more.

From Despair To Hope

With the season seemingly over, the shackles seem to have been released from City, and the early-season free scorers returned, in part helped by Tevez returning to the fold. But as watched City comfortably beat West Brom 4-0, news came through - United we're losing at Wigan.

Damn you City and United I thought, tongue in cheek. I had accepted the season was over, and now I was being drawn back in, getting my hopes raised, only for the inevitable to happen, namely for them to be dashed again.

United lost. The lead was back down to five points. Pleasing, but it wouldn't make any difference, with an easy home game against Aston Villa coming up next for them.

Football Myth

Tottenham Hotspur are the great entertainers

No, no, no. Nyet. Nien. Non. Nae. No. Of course it depends on your definition of "entertainers", but the fact is that for the last two seasons they have scored fewer goals than Manchester City in total, and also split down have scored fewer goals at home and fewer goals away. They have conceded more too, both in total, and home and away, so maybe this counts as part of being great entertainers. Their record against the rest of the "Top 6" is terrible, their goal difference is 27 goals worse than Manchester City's, 16 worse than Manchester United's, they've scored fewer goals than "struggling" Arsenal. And yet journalist after journalist proclaims that they are playing the best football in the country.

There's no doubt they are an entertaining team, due to their pace, and width, with a number of flair players who are comfortable on the ball. They are great entertainers – they are not THE great entertainers.

As for me: early on Saturday morning, a trouble-free drive saw a group of us in a Norwich pub by 10:30am. The atmosphere was relaxed. Grand National bets were placed, and soon the game was upon us.

City excelled, romping to a 6-1 victory, Tevez helping himself to a hat trick. Aguero scored two magnificent goals. Tevez's golf swing celebration was a disgrace - his knees were bent and he pulled through the ball too much - he'd be lucky to stay on the fairway. The young lad behind me thought everything Silva did was "sick", a bit harsh, but we're all entitled to our opinions. The home crowd were magnificent, staying to the end, and providing excellent company afterwards. The test of the day was a blur.

As expected, United best Aston Villa easily, helped by Ashley Young providing a diving master class. Another of Alex Ferguson's wine club had turned up to Old Trafford to have their bellies tickled, before rolling over. A youthful side from Alex McLeish ensured United didn't even have to break into a sweat.

So the gap was 5 points, with only four games to go now. Time was running out. United would have the chance to go 8 points clear when they faced Everton, as City faced Wolves later in the day.

I couldn't bear to watch the United match. They were going to win, so what was the point? Twitter was telling me Everton were playing well. It still wasn't going to make any difference. But then Everton scored. Hmm. A glimmer of hope in our season, nothing more. I turned the game on, then off again - too nervous. The inevitable equaliser came, and as the second half progressed, United took the lead. It was good while it lasted. Friends came round to watch the City match.

We decided to go to the pub. 3-1 United, game over. At the pub, I checked the score. 4-2. Still game over then.

We had a couple of drinks, and the masochist in me decided to check the score. Everton had scored. Surely not? A few more sips. Checked again. My word- 4-4. Five minutes and Fergie time- they would still win, jammy buggers. Palpitations. I refreshed the web page every 10 seconds. Time slowed down to a near halt. What seemed like an eternity later, I saw the most wonderful two letters of the season -FT. This was back on.

At that moment, I experienced the last workings of a settled digestive system for at least 3 weeks. The nerves had started to kick in.

City did their job at Wolves, immense relief felt when Nasri settled the game. It was amazingly back in City's hands (and United's, if that makes sense).

United have the experience. They've been there, done it, bought the T-shirt. They are stronger over the second half of the season.

Not quite. The club has the experience. The likes of De Gea, Young, Welbeck, Jones or Smalling certainly don't. It was squeaky bum time. And the Manchester Derby was suddenly taking on an importance I had never before experienced.

I needed a lie down.

Football Myth:

<u>Manchester United are stronger over the second half of the season</u>

Well strictly speaking, there is some truth in this. But not as much as you might think. Since football began in 1992, United have averaged 40.5 points in the first half of seasons, and 42.3 points in the second half of seasons. So there is an increase in the second half, but it isn't much really, under two points.

What this tells us more than anything perhaps is that they are consistent. And as much as they may or may not improve at the "business end" (yuk) of the season, it may be as much a case of them keeping going whilst those around them often falter (I'm looking at you Kevin Keegan). Of course you must also factor in points lost due to dead rubbers at the end of seasons, so there is an improvement, but it's not a huge swing in form.

I still had little confidence. We would still have to overcome two huge obstacles to win the league. It was still advantage United. But at least United couldn't win the league at the Etihad. Small mercies and all that.

And as I wrote that week, all of Sky's dreams had come true.....

The Sky Hype Machine

The thing about obituaries is that it is better to publish them after the subject has died. Two weeks ago, Manchester United were the champions in all but name. T-shirts had been printed to celebrate their 20th title, a United-supporting bookmakers had paid out on them, endless articles were being written about Roberto Mancini's future, and the season was fizzling out, as City blew their unassailable five-point lead (eight if you write for a tabloid, ten if you're Mark Lawrenson on Football Focus. Five if you like to deal in facts). There were rumours that when the two teams met on 30th April, City players would have to form a guard of honour for the United team. At the very least, United could clinch the title at their neighbour's ground.

Not any more. United have wobbled twice over the past fortnight, and a door has opened. The lead is down to three points, and if City win the Manchester Derby next week, they will go top of the table. As will be mentioned later, that is only half the story, but it certainly a surprising turn of events.

Elsewhere, Everton's wholly unexpected comeback against United on Sunday was the greatest news Sky Sports have ever had. Their spring blue riband event, stupidly positioned on a Monday night, had seemingly turned into a damp squib. Now, it's all systems go. Advertising space will be at a premium, the dollars will roll in, the hype machine has had new batteries put in, and will have seriously overheated by this time next week.

And already Sky have hyped the game beyond comprehension. Think the last days of Rome, couple that with a World Cup Final, mix with the Rumble in the Jungle, add a dash of the last day of the Ryder Cup and garnish with a selection of the greatest penalty shoot outs. Magic Mega Manchester Mash-up Monday is only days away. Or Mancini Meltdown Monday if City lose their nerve, or he waves an imaginary yellow card. New montages are being prepared as we speak, moody images of both managers aligned to a bombastic soundtrack, as two gladiators go to war, to the death, winner takes all, there can be no prisoners, it's the clash of the titans, the biggest game in Premiership history, the dawning of a new era, it's a......sorry about that.

A hundred players will be wheeled out to vomit forth endless banalities about the upcoming match. The buzzwords will be experience, pressure, and history. The United players have been gagged (but not the ex-players, sadly), the focus is intense. The announcement of the match referee is headline news. Desperate attempts are made via social media sites to get Yaya Toure banned because he may have raised two fingers at some opposition fans 80 yards away. Either way, I've bought some Immodium (Plus), and picked up my beta blockers. It's going to be a nervy week, and a nerve-shredding night.

In reality, not THAT much has changed. City are 2/1 for the league now, having been 12/1 just a couple of weeks ago. A couple of weeks before that, they were 1/2. United are still favourites, and rightly so. Whilst many a City fan may now proclaim that the title is now in City's hands, it is also in United's, so it's a pointless cliché. If City should win next Monday, they then have to do it all again, beating Newcastle away, unless United slip up against Swansea or Sunderland, which despite the last fortnight, seems unlikely. City may well have to win two cup finals, and then meet a team fighting for its premiership life, led by their ex-manager, on the last day of the season. At least United will play two teams with little to play for, their summer holidays already booked, their minds already on that lovely beach in Antigua.

Normally, it would be correct to talk now about swings in momentum, in confidence, and balances of power. We were assured that United had the experience, had been there and done it, and would cruise over the finishing line. That's what I thought too. But there have already been too many swings to know what lies ahead. It only takes a mis-timed tackle or a bad refereeing decision to cause another seismic swing. It becomes harder to call when you consider City's lengthy troubles away from home, and the fact that even as United accumulated win after win, their performances were distinctly average (at times). Who is in better form now? It's a grey area.

Now it is down to the managers as much as the players. Mancini surely knows that a win is vital, and must stick with his two free-scoring Argentineans up front. But then again, a draw leaves a slim chance of title glory, a loss none at all. As for Ferguson, he'd probably be happy with a draw, leaving the title in United's hands with a good cushion, but can you set up a team to get a draw? He's unlikely to do that. And for the losers, the ultimate punishment – a Sky interviewer acting like a moron and asking the worst questions possible. Andy Burton thinks nothing of asking Carlos Tevez if he has dived when replays showed he had his ankle stamped on. A Sky interviewer feels no shame in trying to make Terry Connor cry. Geoff Shreeves thinks it's acceptable to tell Ivanovic live on air he will miss the Champions League final. The stakes are high on Monday – the chance to avoid these buffoons.

Thankfully Chelsea have dug deep in the Camp Nou and out-hyped anything Monday could bring. The attention will rightly be theirs for a good couple of days. Sometimes the hype is justified, sometimes the game gives you amazing nights like Chelsea fans experienced this week. They too were written off, a team on their last legs months ago. Now they could win two trophies. A funny old game indeed. On Monday the game might well be a dour one, the hype more about the consequences of the result rather than the quality of match expected. Either way, the atmosphere will be electric, the footballing world watching on. Let's hope it at least partly lives up to the billing.

The Run-In To End All Run-Ins

Derby days are, of course, horrible. I have never felt as ill before a match as I did on 30th April.

And yet City's recent history has given me a huge dilemma regarding my hatred of all things derby day. Without derby days, I would not have experienced our FA Cup semi-final win at Wembley. I would have missed out on the staggering 6-1 win at Old Trafford. I'd have never experienced the euphoria of full-time at the Derby on 30th April 2012.

On the plus side, I'd also have darker hair.

Before the derby, I drank 3 pints in 3 hours. It was a struggle to do that. People kept talking to me, but I had nothing to say. This was the definition of torture – water-boarding, or having Kula Shaker blasted into your ears 24 hours a day for 6 years would be a breeze compared to this.

To sum up, I just wanted it over.

But then I saw the United line up, and it finally dawned on me. Alex Ferguson is now scared of City's squad. The line up was one to try and nullify City - the tables had finally been turned.

The match itself needs no new words from me. City were better throughout. United didn't muster a single shot on target. And for the first time in my lifetime, I wasn't flatlining with anxiety at the thought of a late United goal - they never threatened. Full time, and City somehow found themselves back at the top of the table. And here are some old words, written the day after.

It was billed as the biggest game in Premiership history. A potential audience of 600 million people were to tune in to watch the two Manchester clubs go head to head for the title for the first time in over forty years. It is debatable if this was the biggest games since 1992, when the Premier League age dawned.

After all, Chelsea went to United in a similar position last season as City found themselves pre-match on Monday. The difference here was that City had home advantage, and this was a derby. A week of nerves, taunts and bravado boiled down to this, and as it turned out, it was the most-watched match in Premiership history.

As with all big games, it attracted a celebrity crowd. Michel Platini was rumored to be trying to make it to the match, Diego Maradona was definitely there, along with Liam Gallagher, who gate-crashed the post-match press conference. Ex-chairman Thaksin Shinawatra sat in amongst the fans, and ex-players Shaun Goater and Shaun Wright Phillips were given back-stage passes. Even Eden Hazard was there, watching his potential suitors. The rain thankfully stopped for a day, as Manchester was magically transformed into a sunny paradise (of sorts). The stage was set, and the atmosphere was electric.

For all the hype, the match was unlikely to live up to the billing, due to the high stakes and the tension that inevitably tags along. But perhaps the telling moment occurred not during the match, but an hour before it even began, when the team line ups were announced. City went with an unchanged line up from the side that had beaten Wolves 2-0 the previous week. United however, went with a line up that had not been seen before, and appeared almost to be an acceptance by Alex Ferguson that United couldn't go toe-to-toe with City.

Was it also an admission that years of Glazer management had left him with an inferior squad? Before the match, Ferguson had stated that he would never send out a team to play for a draw, but here was a line-up that appeared to contradict that – and so it proved. In the end, it turned out to be the first game in three years in which United had not registered a single shot on target.

On the touchline too, Ferguson was showing signs of a changed man. Like many a manager, he is well-known for having the odd word or a hundred in the ear of the fourth official, but it is rare that he has a touchline spat with an opposing manager, especially one with whom he is known to have an amicable relationship.

And whatever happens in the final two games of the season (and it is still hanging in the balance), there were more signs on Monday night that times are changing. Last season's FA Cup semi-final and the 6-1 demolition of United at Old Trafford had helped remove a feeling of fear that past City teams may have felt when facing United. Even when United were victorious at the Etihad Stadium in the FA Cup in January, the second half 10-man 2 goal comeback had United rattled when at half-time it looked like they could emulate that earlier 1-6 score-line. David Silva in fact said as much after the match on Monday – the psychological hold United had over City has gone.

For City, the title race is now firmly back in their hands. However, it is too early to be celebrating with a daunting trip to Newcastle on the horizon. With United playing two teams with little to play for, and City finishing the season against a QPR team desperately fighting against relegation, there is plenty of work to be done. Roberto Mancini has laid the groundwork by annoying the Sunderland manager Martin O'Neill, a deliberate act designed to ensure that both teams United face will try and prove him wrong and show that for United these are not easy games as Mancini has claimed.

But whatever happens, this is a new Manchester City. The old City raised the hopes before dashing them cruelly. The old City would have lost the FA Cup semi-final last season (or gone one better and lost the final instead). The old City would have seen its season end with a whimper, or at least surrender the title at home to their fiercest rivals. When City held a five point lead at the top of the table, and were destroying opposition teams earlier this season, it seemed this would be their best ever chance to win the title. But come what may, they have overcome psychological hurdles in the past month that should ensure that they can compete for the title season in, season out.

In addition, the constant talk of Ferguson's mind games, along with his squad's greater title-winning experience has proved to be something of an exaggeration. City's squad have won titles themselves, many cups, and a World Cup to boot. This is not new territory for many of them. The City squad contains plenty of players who have dealt with high pressure football before. Balotelli has league titles to his name, as does Edin Dzeko, winning a title with Wolfsburg for the first time.

Gael Clichy won a title as a young man at Arsenal, whilst of course Yaya Toure and Carlos Tevez have been there and done it. David Silva has represented his country on the ultimate stage, and apart from the 40 other trophies that the squad can count between them, it is a team full of internationals who have played in many huge games. Now they have to prove once more that they have what it takes. There may be more twists and turns to come, and the last two days of the football season could yet provide the **greatest climax ever to a Premiership season**.

Just call me Nostradamus. Little did I know just what the end of the season had in store.

The strange thing was that after the Derby, I still felt sick. I nursed a pint in town for over an hour. I couldn't relax, perhaps because I knew the stakes had just been raised even higher, and I had another week of poor sleep and anxiety attacks awaiting me.

I still thought United were favourites. We were going to mess it up at Newcastle weren't we??

It was the usual routine per-match. Few words, anxiety, waves of nausea. Shouldn't chasing titles be more fun than this?

I needn't have worried. City put in the most assured performance of the season. Unlike me, they never panicked. Yaya delivered again when it mattered. We were one game away from the title. Gulp.

Destiny Calling

The week between the Newcastle and the QPR match was the longest of weeks. Strictly speaking all weeks are the same length, it's a constant, but I assure you this particular week was double the length, and then some.

For a few days, I did well to ignore football. I worked hard, read little of the internet, and kept my TV on Dave or Comedy Central. Some time on Thursday I suddenly got that horrible feeling in the pit of my stomach, and after that, I was back to being a wreck.

Everyone else was confident. I heard 4-0 bandied about a lot. I couldn't share such confidence – but what do I know eh? As I approached the ground, a girl was posing with a CHAMPIONS flag. My fears had come true – some City fans were rather getting ahead of themselves. In a savage example of criticism, I tutted quietly, shook my head slightly, and walked on. I doubt the poor girl has ever fully recovered from my rebuttal.

The day had finally come. You know the script by now - anxiety, nausea, and near-catastrophe. You know everything that happened, every moment. The rest is history. Here's what I wrote, in a daze, the day after. It deserves a chapter of its own.

This Is How It Feels To Be City

I sat in my seat with a hollow feeling the like of which I had never experienced before. This was worse than a derby defeat, this was worse than relegation. Manchester City had managed to let me down again, they had managed to snatch away all my hope and expectancy, to leave me wondering for the millionth time why I put myself through this year after year. All the football insecurities I had carried around with me like a drenched duffel coat since David Pleat skipped across the Maine Road turf had returned. Why always me?

There was little anger around me in the ground, just shock and dejection. A stunned silence, haunted looks aplenty. The man in front of me stood throughout, but at times I didn't even bother peering past him to watch the match, rooted in my seat as another aimless cross sailed behind the hoardings. The clock sped towards 90, and it was all over, that much was clear. Then, a goal. A clenched fist, but it changed little. Maybe Sunderland could grab a late equalizer, and similarly, maybe Cameron Diaz would drop by the next day and ask me out on a date.

The final whistle was moments away. Almost time to slink home in silence, to sit alone with the television off and ponder how this day that I had built up to all my life could have ended like this. Then I'd have to wake up the next day and instantly be reminded that *they* were champions once more, and I would never be allowed to forget it.

And then…..

………..the noise.

Pandemonium. Unbridled joy, never before witnessed on quite this scale. Bouncing off endless people, hugging strangers, utter chaos, thanking a god I don't believe in, shock, a few tears (high pollen count), and the greatest feeling of relief that I will experience in my time on this planet. Someone punched me in the mouth (accidentally I presume). A quick dental check, no blood. Suddenly, life seemed a whole lot better. Had this really happened? If so, how?

Only City would have done it this way, only they could have made life so ridiculously difficult when a routine victory was expected from the team with the best home record in the division against the team with the worst away record. But because this is how City tend to operate, it gave every City fan a moment that will never be forgotten, which will never be matched.

Moments like yesterday remind us why we love football. Could you imagine life without it? It has so much to answer for. I haven't had a good night's sleep in weeks, I have had bouts of nausea lasting days, and have thought of little else apart from a title race that I had given up for dead only a few weeks ago. Oh to be rubbish again.

Last season's FA Cup triumph and this season's title is payback for suffering spread over three decades, the moment I've waited for since 1982, but many fans never get the chance of such rewards, so I am grateful. However, a promotion, beating your bitter rivals or even a last-minute winner is often enough to keep our faith, to keep us believing. Popular belief over the past few years has led me to believe that City were a universally hated club now, the oil money having hoovered up a merry band of mercenaries in a vain attempt to buy the league. Imagine then my surprise at the many messages of congratulations that I received post-match from fans of all clubs. City won fans yesterday because the day presented football at its most compelling, it showed why it is the greatest sport, perhaps why the Premier League is the most entertaining league. Every neutral would have reacted to what happened in some form or other. And as for United, well we always like to see the most successful side knocked off its perch, it's part of our national identity, and just means they have been rather successful in the past.

Now, every monkey has been removed from City's once-massive back. The first Premiership title is always the hardest to win, just like the first trophy was so hard to achieve before last season. In one respect the pressure is lifted slightly now, but it will be just as hard to retain the title now, and Mancini will be expected to make an impact in Europe too.

The celebrating went on late into the night. Heaving, clammy bars were stripped dry, songs were sung throughout, and the fans staggered home content and exhausted in the pouring rain, for this is Manchester. The neighbours were very noisy indeed.

I woke up today with a sunburnt forehead and a bruise on my shin the size of a melon. I watched Match of the Day three times, I watched Aguero's goal at least ten times (with commentary in three different languages). I bought every newspaper. I devoured Twitter and Facebook, and the football message boards. I laughed at Paul Merson's meltdown on Soccer Sunday, and, because football is a cruel world sometimes, took a guilty pleasure in watching the United fans at Sunderland react to our winning goal. I watched Sky sports, I watched Match of the Day again, I wrote this blog.

The smile will remain for days, even a six-hour training course tomorrow can't stop that, but the smile is mostly for others too – the great friends that any football fan gets to share such days with, and the lasting memories that go with that. It's for the great ambassadors at the club who have truly earned this trophy, such as Mancini, Silva, Aguero, Richards and Aguero, and the backroom staff too, like Life President Bernard Halford, who has served the club for over 50 years.

The sun is shining once more, and it's time to go into the centre of Manchester and watch the best City team I've had the pleasure to follow parade the Premiership trophy round the streets of the city. Manchester City, 2011/12 Premier League Champions. Blimey. This is how it feels to be City.

The Aftermath

By Wednesday, I had read the whole of the internet. The feeling of euphoria hadn't died down. When I went into work on the Tuesday I was treated like a returning war hero - you'd think I had scored the winning goal. And one extra thought struck me after another marathon session on YouTube. In the seconds, then minutes after THAT goal went in, my friends around me in that stadium were at that moment the most important people in my life and in the world. They were all my best friends, and we were all experiencing something so special it will never be forgotten, it will never be matched. Soppy, but true.

We'll always have that glorious afternoon in Beswick. God bless football. Eventually, you always remind me why I love you so. Now let's make it more than once every blue moon.

It's all downhill now of course. Chelsea are strengthening their team at some pace. United too are spending. Talk of City dominating the English game is poppycock. But it's downhill because City can never match what happened on 13th May 2012. Winning the league, for the first time in 44 years, against your fiercest rivals, on goal-difference, with two goals in injury-time. I don't want them to beat that!

We'll never win 6-1 at Old Trafford again. I doubt we'll tonk Spurs 5-1 at White Hart Lane either.

And in my mind, there is a link between the 6-1 win at Old Trafford, and City winning the league. You see, the title win secured the 6-1's special place in City's history. If City had blown the league and let United in to win their 20th Championship, then yes, the result would of course stand, the stats would show it as the biggest victory since before any of us were born, but it would be tainted. It would have been almost useless, as it didn't help deliver the title. As it turned out, it now has a special part in a momentous season. The wonderful memories of that day can remain intact, and untainted by subsequent failure.

Bits & Bobs

Premiership Season Review

It may not have been the highest quality, but it was certainly one of the most entertaining seasons in living memory, with the most amazing climax. In the end, Manchester City claimed their first top-level title in 44 years, beating Manchester United on goal difference, whilst Arsenal claimed third place, neighbours Spurs finishing in fourth, pipping a gallant Newcastle to a Top 4 Spot. No Premier League title has ever been decided on goal difference before, and it is only the 6th time the top division has been decided this way.
At the other end of the table, Wolves went down with a whimper after the sacking of Mick McCarthy, and were eventually joined by Steve Kean's Blackburn Rovers and Bolton Wanderers, who ended an 11 year run in the top division. In between, and the three promoted teams stayed up, only the second time this has ever happened.

Here's a look at the hi and lowlights of the season:

Early Season Madness:
Manchester United 8 Arsenal 2, Tottenham Hotspur 1 Manchester City 5, Manchester United 1 Manchester City 6. Were defenders taking the season off? Well no, nothing had changed really, It was a momentary lapse in the space-time continuum, and soon we returned to normal. Well except for Arsenal 5 Tottenham 2, Manchester United 4 Everton 4, Chelsea 3 Arsenal 5, or…..

Racism & Off The Field Controversy
This was the season when much of the talking points revolved around events away from the kicking of a football. Whilst Carlos Tevez was busy reducing his golf handicap, this was also the year of racism scandals. The biggest domestically came at the end of the year as Luis Suarez was banned for eight games for racist comments made towards Patrice Evra.

The row rumbled on as Liverpool refused to accept their lot, but with John Terry due in court after the Euros, the topic is going to remain in the news. If only everyone had taken Sepp Blatter's advice and shaken hands at the end of the match – problem solved. Needless to say, Anton Ferdinand and Patrice Evra were portrayed as the guilty parties in all of this by some of the cretins that reside in our green and pleasant land, and death threats inevitably followed.

Tragedy

The end of 2011 also plunged the world of football into deep shock, as Gary Speed took his own life. It was a story that people struggled to comprehend, a man who seemingly had it all, but it turned out didn't. A reminder, along with the tragic death of Gary Ablett in the New Year, that it is only a game. It will never be more important than life or death. Never had a disputed penalty or a last minute equalizer seemed less important. Football had lost one of the great servants of the Premier League era. At least for Patrice Muamba, there was a happier ending, but the occurrences of natural athletes suffering with heart problems seems to be more problematic than ever before. Italy has some of the most stringent tests in this area. Let's hope the English game follows suit as soon as possible.

Returning Heroes

Paul Scholes and Thierry Henry decided they couldn't stay away, and did their bit in pushing on their respective teams. Even Robbie Keane showed his face again for a short while. What it showed more than anything was that two of the big teams were short on depth of quality to resort to such moves, and whilst talk of Scholes returning to the England team is ludicrous, it also hints at the paucity of talent available to England manager Roy Hodgson.

Tottenham Hotspur and the FA's Role In Their Decline

On the day Harry Redknapp left court a free man, Fabio Capello and the FA called it a day. Fabio got the TV, the house and a few million pounds, but for Redknapp, presumed by the world's media to be Capello's successor, it all went downhill thereafter. Many blamed it on the speculation about the England job distracting Spurs, but it's a weak argument. They thrashed Newcastle before their form fell away, the more likely reason being Redknapp's reliance on key players, who understandably became jaded. In the end, they were relying on a Chelsea Champions League defeat to gain access to next year's competition.

Promotion and Consolidation
Quite an achievement, as all three promoted sides stayed up, and stayed up playing good football. There was no compromise in style, though QPR had the resources to expect a stay in the top league. Either way, they were, and will be, worthy additions to the premier league. Brendan Rogers has turned down an approach from Liverpool, but Grant Holt's transfer request (declined) shows that with success comes a whole new set of problems and challenges.

Another Varied Season For Arsenal
Same old, same old. Some brilliant play, some suspect defending, low points and calls for the manager's head before a resurgence which ultimately left them where they began. This could go on forever, or else at some point Wenger has to compromise on his principles and bring in some established big names, and go for the title. If they don't, we will all be subjected to playground bully Piers Morgan's expert opinions for the next 20 years. And no one deserves that.

Chelsea's Season Of Two Halves
Another big name manager under pressure, who eventually fell on his sword. With hindsight, Villas Boas and his methods seemed doomed from the start, and by the time he left, Chelsea's season resembled a train-wreck. It just goes to show the fine lines in football, as under Roberto Di Matteo, the club have picked up the FA Cup, and tonight will aim to become the first London side to win the Champions League. If they don't, it's the Europa League for them next season. No pressure then.

Never Go Back
Liverpool might go back to Rafa Benitez this summer, but going back to King Kenny ultimately didn't work out. Were they close to usccess or a million miles away? Well Dalglish brought a trophy back to the club, and almost a second, but the league form was far from acceptable, his big money purchases utterly underwhelming, and they finished the season below neighbours Everton. It was a bridge too far for Liverpool's American owners.

He Came From Italy, To Manage Man City
Hard to imagine, but only a month ago, Mancini's job was on the line. Obituaries had been written on him and City's season. Now, he has delivered the first title to the blue half of Manchester in 44 years. A week is a long time in football, and judging by the QPR match, so is 15 seconds.

Awards:

Manager of The Year
How do you choose the best manager? Many think the winner should be the manager of the Champions. Fair enough. All three promoted teams stayed up, so there are merits to choosing Brendan Rogers or Paul Lambert, but for me Alan Pardew is a worthy winner – fighting for Champions League football until the last day of the season, they were a team I expected to struggle for survival after losing key players in the summer.

Player of The Year
Robin Van Persie would be a perfectly acceptable winner, but in the end he was probably pipped by the inspirational Vincent Kompany, who led his team to the title by example, scoring the crucial winner in the Manchester Derby on April 30th.

Biggest Flop
Stewart Downing – it's quite some achievement to have no goals or assists over a whole league campaign (when regularly picked). This led to a million tweets about the sacking of Kenny Dalglish being his first assist of the season. Still, I have vague memories of him scoring against Oldham,

as did Roy Hodgson clearly, who amazingly thinks he's good enough for the England squad.

André Villas-Boas wasn't far behind, but he'll be back, and stronger for it.

Best Goal

Papiss Cissé's second v Chelsea. An astonishing feat to beat a goalkeeper of Petr Cech's quality from that angle, that distance and with a half-volley with the outside of the right foot, though the little voice in my head still insists he just swung his foot and got lucky.

Runner up prizes for Hatem Ben Arfa for Newcastle in a 2-0 win v Bolton in April, and Peter Crouch's volley against Manchester City.

Best Match

Manchester City 3-2 QPR. What more could you ask for? Great goals, defensive howlers, red card madness, the risk of relegation, then being saved from relegation, the lead changing hands three times, an injury-time comeback and a title won with the last kick of the season. Not bad, when all said and done. Other contenders can be found in the high-scoring madness mentioned earlier.

And In The End…

And on the 7th day, god created a Manchester City title – a true miracle. Steve Kean is still in a job, but many more fell at the hurdles. A crazy season full of talking points delivered right to the end. It wasn't always pretty, it wasn't always pleasant, but it was never boring.

Player Ratings

Joe Hart – 9

Probably England's goalkeeper for the next 10 years at least, Hart has firmly established himself as one of the Premier League's best goalkeepers. For the second season in succession he won the Golden Gloves award for the most clean sheets. Not the finished article, but he rarely put a foot wrong.

Gael Clichy – 8

A bargain buy like much of Manchester City's defence for £7m last summer from Arsenal, Clichy had an excellent season, helping fill a position that has been a problem for City for decades. Quietly gone about his job, and has been a reliable pick down the left, despite the warnings from Arsenal fans about his various failings.

Aleksander Kolarov – 6

As frustrating as ever, an expensive acquisition that has failed to deliver. Hammer of a left-foot, but lacks pace, and defensive reliability. Could be better served being moulded into a left-sided midfielder, but more likely to move on. However, when standing in for Clichy, he rarely let the side down.

Vincent Kompany – 10

What more can be said? A vastly accomplished defender, he has grown in stature season-by-season. Hardly ever makes a mistake, a wonderful captain, and a statesman off the pitch. An excellent ambassador for the club, how fitting that he got the winning goal in the crucial recent Manchester Derby. Badly missed when suspended in January.

Joleon Lescott – 9

Manchester City's most improved player over the past 18 months, it is staggering that he is constantly overlooked for the England squad. City won 81% of games with him in the side, and 43% without him. Almost ruined a perfect season on the last day, but it was the only mistake he has made in recent months. He finally looks like a £20m+ player.

Stefan Savic – 5

In a team full of accomplished players, Savic was the obvious whipping boy for the City fans. Manchester City won every game with him in the side until defeat at Swansea in March, but his season was characterised by nervy performances, beginning with the nervy 302 win at QPR last autumn. Young, and a full international, he has time on his side, but questionable if he will be given that time at City.

Kolo Toure – 5

A wasted season for the Ivorian, having served a drug ban for taking his wife's slimming pills, then exiting for the African Cup of Nations, and his limited appearance in the first team were adequate but unspectacular. Not the player he was, he has no real future at the club except perhaps as a reason for Yaya Toure to stay at City.

Micah Richards – 8

A great season as he has continued to knuckle down and progress as a player. Great threat going forward, but still constantly overlooked by England managers due to perceived poor positional sense and lack of balance. Still needs to work on game, but has had a great season, and is passionate about club and country.

Pablo Zabaleta – 8

Almost a 9/10 season, Zabaleta is Manchester City's cult hero player. Great season, to the extent that he kept Micah Richards out in the run-in – utterly dependable, committed, never moans and whilst not the most skilful player in the world, he never lets the team down, and was key in the dramatic victory over QPR.

Midfield

Gareth Barry – 8

The scapegoat for England's constant failings and the engine of the Manchester City team. Unspectacular throughout, with no long range goals, few shots, no last-ditch tackles or goal-line clearances, Barry has had an excellent season as the "water-carrier" who covers the grounds, mops up play, and allows his colleagues to flourish. City play better when he is in the team, and this season has been his best.

James Milner – 6

A disappointing nine months for Milner, who is handicapped by being versatile, and thus not having a fixed position. Had limited opportunities during the season, and when he has appeared has failed to shine. His stats show he played more than I thought, but there is much more to be had from him, but will he get the chance?

David Silva – 9

A generous 9 perhaps, as Silva's form dipped mid-season, probably caused by a persistent ankle injury, but nothing can take away from a magical season from Manchester City's uber-talented playmaker. Helps the midfield to sparkle, the only thing missing from his game is more goals.

Yaya Toure – 9

A beast of a player, who has proved his worth all season long. A scorer of crucial goals, he has bossed the midfield week-in, week-out. Badly missed in January along with Kompany. Versatile too, happy to play in a defensive midfield position, or even central defence.

Samir Nasri – 8

Arsenal fans would have you believe he isn't very good, and a passenger did (as Irish comedian Dara O'Briain did with this article's author only this week). The truth is rather different. Started on fire, with numerous assists during City's explosive early-season sprint, debuting in their 5-1 win at Spurs. Mid-season he had less of an impact, but has grown in stature in recent months and been vital in the run-in as a more than able cover for David Silva and his ankle.

Adam Johnson – 6

Another season of flattering to deceive. A useful substitute, and a scorer of very good goals, Johnson has not progressed sufficiently and added to his all-round game. When he has started games he has generally been disappointing, and his future at Manchester City may well now be in doubt.

Nigel De Jong – 7

A sign of how far City have come. No City fan could possibly imagine a year ago that De Jong would become anything but a crucial first-team player. But for the 2011/12 season, De Jong was often the spare part, spending many a game on the bench. However, in the second half of the season he has forced himself back into the team on occasions, and his inclusion has allowed Yaya Toure to excel in a more advanced role.

Forwards

Carlos Tevez – 5

What is there left to say? Spent much of the season playing golf in Argentina, and when it seemed impossible he had a future at the club he returned, having failed to force a January transfer away. With Balotelli going astray once more, his return and goals (most notably a hat trick at Norwich) were instrumental in City winning the title.

Edin Dzeko – 7

Might be seen as a generous score, but he did score 19 goals. Started the season on fire, before form and his touch deserted him. However, he wasn't helped by being rotated, and Manchester City's style of play doesn't really suit him, and he appears to be a player that requires a run in the side to flourish. However, cameos from the bench late in the season were vital in winning their last two games.

Sergio Aguero – 9

Perhaps a 10? For the goal at QPR alone, legend status is assured, but here was a man of 23 years old, in his debut season in England, scoring 30 goals. And yet he can be even better. Missed quite a few chances, but what a player, and never stops smiling. The fact he was beaten to Young Player of the Year by Kyle Walker is one of life's great mysteries.

Mario Balotelli – 6

An enigma wrapped in a puzzle wrapped in another enigma. Clearly a man of immense talent, Balotelli continued to frustrate. He wasn't helped by ridiculous officiating, and media witch-hunts, but he hardly helped himself anyway. Has time on his side, and showed during the season that he can go right to the top, none more so than in the 6-1 drubbing of Manchester

United at Old Trafford, but he needs to mature, quickly, as City do not need another season of distractions.

Manager Score – Roberto Mancini – 9

A score that many would scoff at, claiming anyone could win the league with the funds available to Mancini. Maybe an 8/10 then, but Mancini dealt with the crazy season that fate threw at him with aplomb. He dealt with his misbehaving strikers, he dealt with the scrutiny, the pressure, and the constant criticism, and he got a team playing better football than anyone else – more clean sheets, fewer goals conceded, more goals scored, and team spirit maintained. And, at the end of the day, he delivered the holy grail – the premier league title. Mission accomplished.

So what were the other highlights of the season? There were plenty to deal with

Game of The Season

It had to be Manchester City 3 Queens Park Rangers 2. Here was a game that had it all – the full range of emotions, great goals, defensive howlers, red card madness, potential shocks, potential relegation, a late comeback and eventually a league champion.

Goal Of The Season

Again, it has to be Manchester City's last kick of the season, and Sergio Aguero's winner against QPR. There were many other wonderful goals, technically better than Aguero's last. Aguero's first away to Norwich, the flowing move that led to Aguero's winner at Arsenal in the Carling Cup, the Silva pass that led to the 6th goal at Old Trafford, Toure's game-changer at Newcastle, Nasri's winner at home to Chelsea, and many, many more.

Player of The Season

Vincent Kompany. A case could be made for at least five players, but Kompany was imperious throughout, and led by example. The best £7m that Manchester City have ever spent.

Stats:

28 league games won - 53% of away games won, 95% of home games won

93 goals for, 29 against - City were the biggest scorers in the country, followed by Sheffield United, who weren't promoted.

14 games unbeaten at start of season.

23 goals from Sergio Aguero

17 assists by David Silva

No goals conceded in first half-hour of any league match all season.

Failed to score in 5 league games.

664 shots on goal in league season.

1. City's final position in the league.

Quotes From The Season

£31m signing Berbatov: "I had the opportunity to sign for City but chose United.City are the champions but to me they just bought the title.

Barry Glendenning's player of the year - Kompany. "One of very few reasons that neutrals might warm to Manchester City."

Dara O' Briain (to me) re: Nasri: we got 3 good months out of him in in 3 seasons. What did you get? 5 goals? Where would he come in your player of the season?

#MUFC chief Gill on #MCFC: "We'll see what's happening with the financial fair play, how that's implemented and what the sanctions are."

@RobHarris: Ominous message from Ferguson at United dinner: "Those Sunderland fans who cheered for City ... we won't forget that."

Ian McGarry: Seven points clear to eight points behind. I very much doubt that Sheikh Mansour will forgive Mancini and retain him as coach.

Terry Christian: our tradition of exciting attacking football is an example to the world and every stride by a man in red is a moral victory.

Clayton Blackmore on manager spat at Manchester Derby: "Ferguson was probably fed up of City players asking for yellow cards all the time"

Oliver Holt: Ok, ok, I know City fans think I banged on too much about Mark Hughes but irrespective of that, surely you deserve better than Mancini.

Manchester United coach Rene Meulendteen, April 2012: "Manchester City don't have a well-balanced team. They only have individuals who play for themselves. You can see that they lack the right team spirit.
"There's no chance of Balotelli playing for Manchester United - a player who gets up to the sort of antics he does has no place at our club. I don't believe Sir Alex would sign a player like Balotelli."

After Arsenal beat Manchester City: John Cross: "If Sunday told us anything, The Emirates is a happier place for Van Persie to be. "

Piers Morgan: Contrary to popular belief, I have huge respect for Arsene Wenger. But 7yrs with no trophy is enough. Time for change. #Arsenal

Mark Ogden article title, April 2012: Is it all getting too much for Manchester City manager Roberto Mancini?

Alan Hansen on MOTD "Balotelli won't start for City again this season." (2 days later he started ahead of Aguero and Tevez.)

Roberto Mancini on Manchester: "You can't live badly in a city where everyone respects the rules & parks their cars in the right place."

Ian McGarry: Govt admits it waived £250bn in tax from UK companies but Harry Redknapp in court for unpaid tax in 180k. Priorities? Justice?

John Barnes: "I believe what's going to happen now is that players won't stay at clubs for so long, especially the foreign players. What Sir Alex Ferguson and Kenny Dalglish are doing is signing players they think will stay for years. Phil Jones, Ashley Young, Stewart Downing and Charlie Adam, they're not going to be looking to move anywhere else. Look at City now with Tevez, and what you get with foreign players who really have no allegiance to the club."

Pete Gill, football365.com : "City, reborn by a cash rejection from a man who has only seen them play twice in person,are a club without history."

Martin Samuel: If Phil Jones impresses in midfield he has the capability to change the English game in the way Desailly changed France.

Ollie Holt: I'd take 5 strikers to Euros: Rooney, Welbeck, Bent, Defoe or Sturridge, Owen. Depends on form for some but we know what MIchael Owen can do.

Ollie Holt: If another manager in charge, Michael Owen would still be in England squad but Capello has always ignored him. That's his loss and sadly it's ours too

Ollie Holt: Aguero will be highest profile signing of summer.. still think Charlie Adam to Liverpool could be best though.

Martin Lipton: Aguero is a gamble, and the wrong man to replace Tevez.

Ollie Holt: Is it acceptable then to change name of team, too? Presuming all in favour of Etihad Stadium would be fine with Etihad City as name of team?

Twitter, 13ᵗʰ May 2012. Some time around 4:50pm.

@MCFC 95. AGUERO SCORES AND WINS THE LEAGUE!!!!!

@MCFC City fans on the pitch! The league is ours!!! UNBELIEVABLE!!!

@sidlowe Unbebloodylievable! Incredible

@101greatgoals THIS IS THE GREATEST THING EVER!!!!!!!!!!!

@Connellhugh Greatest moment in PL football without doubt

@football365 Football. Football. Football

@11tegen11 Oh those poor people who "just don't like football...."

@ACMilandrew Man City. Champions.

2011/12 Premier League Champions - our very own Manchester City.

The end.

Quotes From Previous Years

Simon Hattenstone:

"Arsène Wenger says Manchester City are not in touch with the world, that we're destroying football and the global economy by creating inflationary pressures in deflationary times, that we lack values and have no sense of reality. How dare he?

Very easily, in fact. And **any true** Manchester City fan, however hungry for success, would agree with the Arsenal manager.

Mark Lawrenson:

"At a time when people have been left devastated by the credit crunch, football is in danger of shooting itself in the foot. It would be bad enough during a boom time, but during these tough economic times it is sick. If City do this then they will lose the sympathy and support of fans who will begin to question the morality of how someone can spend that sort of money on a player rather than build a new hospital or pay for some lifesaving medical care. People will turn round and say: 'The world has gone mad. I'm not sure about football any more'. How would you feel if you can't pay the bills while a player your club is on mind-boggling money?"

Gordon Waddell:

When Manchester City sign Kaka, stick it in your diary as the day the people's game died forever. When a footballer is paid enough to keep a factory of 1000 people in wages for a week? In this economic climate?

Kaka's good - great, even - but the Brazilian is human.

That's why his signing has nothing to do with football.

And why it will spell the beginning of the end for a lot of punters.

Kenny Burns:

I CANNOT get my breath with all the talk of Manchester City paying more than £100m for AC Milan's Kaka.

And paying him £500,000 a week.

The world and this country has gone completely mad. It is disgraceful, embarrassing, stomach-turning really.

This kind of money should be saved for throwing around to make star-studded teams on those computer games, not for the real world.

The owners should wake up and smell the coffee. There is a credit crunch on and the country is in meltdown.

Former Met Police commander John O'Connor commenting on the ban for Adebayor after kicking Van Persie:

'I am sure the police will want Adebayor to be made an example of. From a police perspective, Adebayor could have been arrested and then charged with actual body harm for the incident with Van Persie. He would then have faced the prospect of standing trial in court.'"

Steven Howard, The Sun
"Yet City still can't get the mega-stars. Instead, they have been forced to settle for second best. It's David Silva not David Villa. It's Mario Balotelli not Fernando Torres.

The same David Silva who will remember Spain's World Cup-winning triumph in South Africa as the time he lost his place in the starting line-up.

And 20-year-old Balotelli, largely unknown outside Italy and on the bench during Inter Milan's run to Champions League glory.

There are also massive question marks over holding midfielder Yaya Toure (£24m)….."

The Journalists And Bias

Personally if I was a journalist writing about the premier league, I would find it difficult to write impartially on City, and by association, United also. So I did a little experiment, using webchats, twitter, emails and the like. I asked every football journalist I could find the following question:

"Do you think it is possible for sports journalists to write fairly and impartially on football when they support a particular (high profile) team? My experiences suggest not....."

These were the replies, in full. I won't name names, but they all write for national papers, with one exception.

- Good question Howard. As football fans we all have certain teams in our heart. I don't think my lifelong allegiance affects my objectivity when reporting on that team or any rival teams. You may beg to differ....

- I'm professional in the day job. Quite why so many fans are obsessed with what teams journos support is beyond me!"

- It does not matter which team individual writers support. This is like saying you must be pro-police to cover crime. What matters is content and getting the balance right between city and united coverage.

- Depends Howard. If I'm writing a news piece or a match report, then it has to be objective. If it's a piece that clearly marks me as a Liverpool fan, then it does what it says on the tin. Some hide their allegiance, I don't. Anyway, I've been accused of all kinds – being an Everton fan or Man United. Most of my reporters are passionate fans of clubs. Hang on, all of them. We argue and abuse each other but are professional enough that you'd never know from their writing.

- I support Cambridge United so impartiality has never been a problem. Sometimes supporters can be the harshest judges so I don't think that's a specific problem. A bigger issue is probably trying to think and write independently when you are dealing with contacts, individuals you like.

- Although every football reporter goes into journalism with some kind of allegiance, very few stick with it as they progress. From my point of view, the old rivalries disappear when you get to know people and players from other clubs. Similarly, you can find people who work for the club you 'supported' difficult to deal with, so that also helps get rid of loyalties.
A few guys certainly get too wrapped up in England team results, but the vast majority of reporters I know do not allow any allegiances to colour their judgement. At the top end of the profession, you can't get away with club bias. I know many fans think we are all Utd / City / Arsenal / Chelsea fans. I've been accused of being all four, so that sums it up!

- I am a journalist who happens to cover football. So the ethics of informing people of the truth, being accurate, objective, fair, impartial and proving debate, must hold true. Supporting a team doesn't give a journalist a right to express opinions, unsupported by facts or a sound basis. It therefore helps if a sports reporter has been first trained as a news reporter. There is no need for a journalist to make their allegiance to a team known to the public. It serves no benefit to them, the reader or the club. It can only invite criticism from fans. The loss of impartiality affects the credibility of the journalist and that of the media outlet.

- It is an interesting question, and I am not sure that it is possible for any journalist to write completely impartially about a match in a division in which their team competes. Obviously you try to comment as fairly as possible, but journalists, much like every other football fan, will have their prejudices and they will inevitably colour their writing. It just depends on the writer as to how much they can mask the level of their impartiality. Some clearly find it tougher than others!

- Yes of course it's possible. It's part of the journalistic DNA. But not a problem I face because I support Dundee! (thanks to Paddy Barclay for that)

Book Reviews:

Paul Lake: I'm Not Really Here

Paul Lake was the biggest "what if" in Manchester City's recent history. What if he had stayed fit for most of his career? What if he had continued his progress as a player? What if he had become an England regular? What if City could have had him in their defence or midfield for a good ten years? What if? What if? What if?

We will never know. Serious injuries treated badly ensured that. What we fans who prayed for the day he might return did not know was the turmoil that the injuries had caused, and the effects that having your career extinguished can have on a young man's life.

In his new autobiography, I'm Not Really Here: A Life of Two Halves, written with his wide Joanne, Lake describes the enormous highs and lows of playing for his beloved club.

Lake was born in 1968, just after Manchester City's last league title. His love of Manchester City was almost instant, and he grew up obsessed with football. At a young age, he realised he had a natural talent for football – he didn't know why, but things came easily. He made his way from the Denton Youth U12 side (aged just 8), through City's youth sides, under the tutelage of the legendary Tony Book, to a YTS traineeship in 1985, and glory with the youth team, winning the FA Youth Cup against Manchester United in 1986. Inevitably, he was soon in the senior squad, making his first team debut in January 1987. This being City, relegation followed soon after, and Lake was to experience the first of many bitter disappointments. The versatile Lake was soon holding down a permanent 1st team place though, his proficiency across the pitch seeing him wear 8 different shirt numbers in one season.

Soon, Malcolm Allison was calling him "the big talent at Maine Road". And later after a call up to an England training session, Bobby Robson reported back to Lake's favourite manager Howard Kendall that he had earmarked Lake as a future England captain. Naturally fans love a home-grown player, a local lad, and Lake was no different, idolised by all City supporters.

But having missed out on the Italia '90 England squad, it wasn't long into his career the following season as City captain that it all started to go wrong, against Aston Villa. One false move, and his cruciate ligament had snapped.

Not that he knew for some time. City's treatment involved an ice pack for days until the swelling reduced, an X-ray, and running up and down the concrete steps of the Kippax stand. Only when he collapsed in his first proper training session did he see a specialist and learn the truth. The damage had been done.

The following years were painful on many levels, a depressing cycle of rehabilitation, hope, and false dawns as he went on to rupture the ligament a further two times as soon as he returned to competitive football. He spent more time recuperating at Lilleshall than any other player in history. All this changed Lake as a man – the young lively, eager player that lived life to the full spiralled into depression, and withdrew from public life, going to extreme lengths to shun contact with others. As Daniel Taylor's review in the Guardian described it, he was a tormented soul.

It is commendable that Lake came out the other side intact, and rebuilt his life. It is even more commendable that he retained the love for his football club despite the way some at the club treated him – mostly Peter Swales, the only person Lake shows bitterness towards in the book, after he shunned him throughout his fight for fitness and fought sending Lake to America for superior treatment.

That treatment was too late, and at the age of 27, Lake was forced to accept that there was no way back, and retired.

For City fans the book is an eye opener, shedding light on the way the club was run under Peter Swales' stewardship. This was a club that allowed drunks to shout abuse from behind a wire fence during training every morning. That had players doing comedy routines at Junior Blues meetings, and had Eddie Large delivering half-time team talks using a variety of celebrity impressions when City were on the cusp of promotion.

This is not just a book for City fans though. Whilst it also beautifully illustrates the life of a footballer, and such things growing up as Manchester ruled the music world, it is less about playing in football matches and more about what the game means to us all, and the despair and multiple lows when your dreams are snatched from your grasp. It also provides an insight into many other people in the game at that time, such as Bobby Robson, John Barnes, Paul Gascoigne and others.

Paul Lake is 42 now. After retirement he studied physiotherapy and worked on the medical staff of various clubs, even running his own practice too, until in March 2010, when he was appointed Ambassador for Manchester City in the Community.

There will always be curiosity over what could have been, what Lake could have achieved if he had avoided injury, and Lake had plenty of time to mull such things over during those fraught years on the treatment table. He came out the other side, and his account is one of the great sporting books of recent years. The final word can go to The Metro newspaper, who said: "The greatest football autobiography ever written? Unquestionably."

Andy Morrison: The Good, The Mad And The Ugly

When you start off reading a football autobiography, your hopes aren't always that high. Perhaps a few inside stories on players you know, insight into managers, the odd anecdote – the usual stuff. Having said that, nothing quite prepared me for the contents of this book. I had fairly clear memories of Andy Morrison, and his role in the resurgence of Manchester City football club. I knew he liked a drink, that his knees had caused him trouble, and that his role at City didn't last that long for those reasons. Little did I know just what else had gone on in his amazing, and often shocking life.

Morrison was born in Kinlochbervie, a small fishing village of 500 people a 100 miles north of Inverness. He had a happy childhood, but at a young age, took the 750 mile journey south with 3 brothers to Plymouth as his father moved away for work. Morrison clearly fears and respects his father in equal measures. He is described as a tough man who helped shape his son. Soon his parents had split up, but his focus turned towards football, and aged 10, he was selected for Plymouth schoolboys. As he grew older, his football skills developed at Plymouth, but there was a new thing in his life too. Alcohol.

"The booze cured me of my chronic shyness. I felt relaxed and the world was a better place. Drink filled in the void in my life and I knew from that moment on, I had something I could turn to when I need to blot out a memory or just feel better about myself."

And with alcohol came fighting, and lots of it with his elder brother Ian, as they tried to be like their father, who himself wasn't averse to the odd "scrap".

Nights out almost inevitably ended in violence, and the consequences often spread to his football career. The fans didn't mind, as long as he did the business on the pitch, and he was a fans' favourite wherever he went because he was a leader, who always gave his all. He seemed fortunate that various managers gave him second (and third) chances and accepted him for what he was. It was even more fortunate that he didn't end up in prison – fighting even crossed the path of Plymouth football club's hooligan element.

After over a 100 games for Plymouth, Kenny Dalglish surprisingly signed Morrison up at Blackburn as he began building his title-winning side, in 1992. Morrison got few opportunities there though, now a small fish in a big pond. Missing Plymouth, depression began to set in for the first time also. It also marked a cycle of fights with team-mates – the red mist often descended under the influence of alcohol, memories of what happened hazy or non-existent most of the time.

Eventually Morrison moved to Blackpool, experiencing more success, though once more violence reared its ugly head, Morrison narrowly avoiding prison after a fight. On the day he was cleared, the night's celebrations ended with yet another fight, and another escape from the arm of the law.

But on the pitch, a disastrous collapse meant Blackpool blew an almost nailed-on promotion push, and Morrison soon moved to Huddersfield under Brian Horton. It wasn't long before injuries started damaging his career, and a serious knee injury meant he only played sporadically for the Terriers over three seasons.

And then came Manchester City, in 1998. Joe Royle needed a leader in the City dressing room, where morale was rock-bottom in the third tier of English football – the rest is history. Morrison's arrival made all the difference along with a few other shrewd signings, and the season ended at Wembley, and a famous play-off victory over Gillingham.

Soon the knee was controlling his life again though, and Morrison would not feature much more for City – on his return to fitness he made a couple of loan moves to try and reach his previous levels of performance, even returning briefly to Blackpool, but his career was effectively over, and eventually he was forced to retire.

Life didn't get any simpler though. Cashing in his pension early on retirement landed him in court once more, this time for benefit fraud. His younger brother was lost to a drug overdose, his brother's propensity for violence led him to prison with a conviction for manslaughter, and his wife had to have a cancerous growth removed – three events that happened within a mere six-month period. And Morrison's link to violence hadn't ended either – after turning out for a pub team, a barrage of abuse by three opposition players led to him following them to a pub post-match and wreaking his own brand of revenge.

But somehow he survived, turning his hand to management, and that is how he found himself on the management team at Northwich Victoria, and now in the Welsh Premier League with Airbus UK.

The book stands well against other footballers' autobiographies, the bland, featureless tomes of recent years having been replaced by a raft of good stories like this or Paul Lake's. Morrison's book does not tug at the heart-strings like Lake's and isn't as professionally written or as polished, but it is still excellently styled, and pulls no punches, written in an honest, straight-forward manner. Never has the word candid been more apt. There's so much in there that no incident gets more than a page of comment, so in a book that is not overly-long, you are pushed along on a roller-coaster ride. Morrison does not hold back, his honesty resulting in great criticism of many famous names from the past twenty years of British football, and plenty of praise too. Clearly Joe Royle is the man that he respects more than any other, as it is he who provides the foreword to the book, showing the feeling was mutual.

There are also little gems in there, like the time Shaun Wright Phillips tried to fight him after a bruising first training session together, and who could forget him getting sent off for licking Stan Collymore's ear? He even ended up at Philosophy School after Willie Donachie helped him to try and defeat his demons. He also ended up in Antigua, coaching youngsters.

Like Lake's book, it is not just about football, it at times is barely about football. This is the man who has been charged with a Section 18, wounding with intent, GBH (twice), affray, actual bodily harm ,threatening behaviour, and many public order offences. Morrison does not have to have played for your club for the book to be of interest. In the end, the football is skimmed over much of the time, a backdrop to the craziness of his personal life. At times you feel the relief when you read four pages without anything bad happening to him – but with the anxiety that comes with knowing another fall is just round the corner.

It's hard not to like Morrison at the end of it all, despite feeling guilty for doing so considering all the wrongs his life has contained. I guess that's often the way when a story is told from one man's perspective. But he does not seek to excuse many of his actions, just to explain why his life has taken its particular path. Whatever you think of the man, it's an interesting read. And let's hope that he has at last found some peace in his life so that the sport that made his name can provide for him for the foreseeable future. This is an autobiography that is a cut above most you will read.

Obituary: Gary Speed

There is so little that can be said, or written, to explain the news that popped up on my television screen on Sunday morning. In a desensitized world, little seems to shock me any more, but the death of Gary Speed was one of those rare times. As the Guardian commented, it was one of those "stop all the clocks" moments.

When someone dies, there is the need to highlight the good points of that person, to pick out their achievements, to paper over the cracks. There was no problem doing this with Speed, because we were dealing with a man that no one, absolutely no one, had a bad word about. I know nothing of him personally apart from what I saw on a television screen, but the consensus from those who did know him was clear: we are dealing with a man who went out his way to help others, was a true gentleman, and was a giant of the Premiership era. With a wife, two young sons, a successful career bringing Welsh football out of the doldrums, and Hollywood looks to boot, he appeared to us to have it all – but we were wrong.

I haven't witnessed such an outpouring of grief and shock from the death of a football man, of any man, in recent years. This spread beyond Welsh football fans and fans of the clubs he wore the shirt of, though their grief will be harder to cope with.

Swansea and Aston Villa made the difficult decision to play their game just hours after the terrible news broke, Shay Given was in tears, as were many others, a minute's silence breaking out into spontaneous support. Craig Bellamy was withdrawn from the Liverpool squad for their match against Manchester City by manager Kenny Dalglish, Bellamy known to be in awe of the Wales manager who had done so much for his career. Howard Wilkinson too was on the phone, struggling to put his grief into words. There was an impeccable minute's silence too at Anfield, not only for Speed, but for the tragic loss of Brad Jones' son, taken by leukaemia at the tender age of five. And as I watched on in my local, the pub fell virtually silent – that spoke more of Speed's legacy than any words I can offer.

But let's remember the man. He gained 85 caps for Wales – only Neville Southall had more. He made 677 senior appearances for Leeds United, Everton, Newcastle United, Bolton Wanderers and Sheffield United during a 22-year career, most notably part of that championship winning Leeds side – the only trophy he would pick up. He was a tenacious midfielder, not merely a jack of all trades, but a master of many. Howard Wilkinson spoke of his versatility, commenting that he had played him in virtually every position bar in goal – he would never let his team down, a consummate professional performing to a high standard long after most would have called it a day. Good players don't always make good managers, but Speed was turning around the Welsh national side. There was an optimism not felt for many years as he nurtured a new wave of youngsters towards some impressive recent results. There was a real feeling that qualification for future World Cup and Euro finals was now a realistic target. And thus it is incomprehensible that the man sat in the Football Focus studio laughing and joking and reminiscing was twenty-fours later no longer with us.

The obvious comment is that it puts everything into perspective – it shames us to have our petty squabbles about whether it was worthy of a yellow card, how bad the referee was, or how much Suarez dives. But whilst the sentiment is true, these minutiae of the sport are an essential part of what makes it the most popular game in the world.

There is no evidence to suggest that Speed took his life because of any link to depression, but I still feel the need to mention it in the week that Stan Collymore laid bare the ravages of the illness. John Gregory once commented that Collymore had nothing to be depressed about, a perfect example of the ignorance of what depression is and how it affects these unfortunate enough to succumb to its destructive path. Collymore went overnight from 8 hours sleep each day to eighteen. He spoke of being fit and healthy one day, mind, body and soul withering and dying the next – he once spent a month in bed.

Much has been done off the pitch to support those who choose football as a profession, and much more needs to be done. Depression does not pick out the poor, the unemployed, the ill. It can pick out anyone. We all have a preconception of footballers having it easy, and many do, relatively speaking. But that is a different argument to that of depression – money cannot keep the demons away. And the support must remain after the playing career ends, as this can be a terrible time for a player who knows nothing else.

Football is a world of machismo and testosterone where you can't admit to frailties, as it shows weakness. You can't admit to being gay, you can't admit to being depressed, you can't admit to being anything other then perfect. Of course you can really, but it is made very, very hard, and it is no wonder many hide their feelings, their sexuality, and more. This has to change. If anything good can come out of tragedies like this, then the sport must shed this image and catch up with other sports, with other walks of life. Robert Enke was a master at keeping his feelings hidden. The book A Life Too Short by Ronald Reng is a moving and harrowing account of the German goalkeeper's constant battle against depression. The support structure needs to be there in football to help people like him, like Collymore, like Justin Fashanu.

People often use such terrible occurrences to show their displeasure at other footballers. Graham Poll disgustingly used Speed as a stick with which to beat Mario Balotelli on Talksport, stupidly sinking to even criticising his hairstyle. Similar ire has been directed towards Carlos Tevez, seemingly the antithesis of Speed, representing everything that Speed would have found deplorable. But we must be careful. I, like most City fans, have expressed my disgust at the antics of our rogue Argentinean striker, but who are we to know what goes on in his private life? Who are we to criticise the club's handling of the whole affair towards a man we know to have family issues? Perhaps we shouldn't be so quick to judge after all. Refusing to walk onto a football pitch was portrayed by me and many more as the ultimate betrayal – perhaps sometimes we football fans need a tad more perspective.

The fact is that we don't know why Speed took his life, and we have no right to know. But sadly the newspapers will dig until they find out, and inflict more pain on a family who have already suffered way beyond what I can comprehend. Already they are pulling apart his final hours, desperate for answers. The family bear the brunt, hence their call for privacy. Our thoughts should be with them, and I hope they can one day move on. No parent wants to bury their child. No child wants to grow up without his or her parents. I hope that Speed's family can take at least some comfort from the tributes pouring in from around the world.

Rest in peace Gary.

Articles From The Archives

Life Without Football

A couple of months ago I was reading an utterly tedious article by Christina Patterson in The Independent – it was one of those pieces that crops up now and again where someone who doesn't like sport prattles on about how boring and pointless sport is, on this occasion describing football as being some men who *chase each other up and down, and sometimes shout, and sometimes scream, and sometimes wave their arms, and sometimes kick a ball.*

And apparently the whole day itself is horrible she says - it takes you hours to get there, because the traffic is awful, and you can't find anywhere to park, and you have to queue for hours in the freezing cold just to get into the stadium, and you have to be herded by police as if you've committed a crime, which you haven't, but now feel like doing, and then when you finally get to your seat, which isn't very comfortable, and the men come out on the stage, wearing outfits that aren't really warm enough for the weather, they don't do anything interesting like sing, or dance, or recite poems.

Apart from the tiresome attempts by some people who don't follow sports, or just particular sports to denigrate those who do, and the total ignorance they show of why we do what we do, it got me thinking – what's it like to not follow sport?

Being a Manchester City fan, the thought has occasionally entered my head over the years that life would be so much easier if I just didn't follow football. And easier still if I didn't follow sport at all. I wasn't being serious of course, but there have been many days that would have been vastly improved without the stress and anguish that city have brought to proceedings.

But boy would I be bored.

I don't think anything brings people together like sport does. Few things provoke such fierce debate and differing opinions. Nothing else provides such a rollercoaster ride, such a sea-change of emotions in such small periods of time.

My mood at the weekend used to rely entirely on City's result. Thankfully, considering those results, I have managed to take a step back and realise that there are more important things in life. Sorry Bill Shankly, but there just are.

90% of my sporting life is taken up by football – of that 95% is taken up by Manchester City. Club beats country, comfortably.

But other sports still provide me with amazing experiences, and without the stress of following football, and the emotional attachment I have to it. The Ashes Series, the Ryder Cup, the 2003 Rugby Union World Cup Final, that time when there was an interesting Formula 1 race. The Grand National, and of course, the Boat Race (OK, maybe not).

Imagine the boredom without sport –There'd be no shouting abuse at the Sunday Supplement panel. No head in hands as Paul Merson tries to pronounce the name of West Brom's right-back. No tweet arguments with John Cross at the Mirror, or telling Stan Collymore to shut up.

No shaking your head at The Sun's player ratings, no articles like this (every cloud and that…), no excitement and expectancy on transfer deadline day, slowly turning to disappointment and regret at taking the day off work (I only did it once, ok?!). No long-odds bet coming in and paying for your weekend. No praying for a good game for Luke Young because you've put him in your Fantasy Football team, or checking the papers to see if Ricardo Fuller has shaken off that niggling thigh injury.

No office debates with the blinkered United fan in the office.

No utter despair, no amazing highs, memorable nights with friends and amazing journeys, home and abroad. No memorable nights in ~~Barcelona~~ Lincoln.

You haven't lived until you have experienced the joy of a penalty shootout victory. Or a last-minute winner. A victory against the odds. A chicken balti pie heated to the temperature of lava. You haven't truly experienced life's rich tapestry until you have paid £8 for a revolting cheeseburger outside Villa Park (I can still taste it now). Or sung with 3000 other people about the referee's suspect parentage.

How would I fill my time without sport? I imagine I'd watch even more rubbish TV, or do really constructive things with my life, but where's the fun in that?

The main problem would be weekends – I could, I think survive the week without sport, at a push. But weekends are a different matter. I'd have to go shopping and round B & Q. I'd probably end up in garden centres or in a coffee shop every Saturday.

Sport is an excuse to drink, should an excuse be needed. It's an excuse to be prejudiced and something of a hypocrite. It occasionally results in you wearing clothes you really shouldn't wear. It makes you swear more than is advisable. It can bring an emotion that no drug can replicate.

It's also about hope – of what good times might lie around the corner. Imagine if I had known 30 years ago when I started supporting City that in the subsequent three decades City would not win a single thing – would I have stopped supporting City there and then? It's possible, however much we say we don't do it for the glory and silverware.

Sadly sport, and usually football, is also an excuse for people who don't like it to pretend they like it for some sort of gain, usually political, or to make them look hip and cool, and part of the gang.

Never is this more apparent than at a world cup or euro finals when suddenly people who haven't seen a football game for 2 years want to talk to you about Wayne Rooney and Rio Ferdinand.

Christina Patterson did get one thing right - football *made men who were sometimes quite sensible, and who sometimes even seemed quite intelligent, behave in ways that seemed quite strange. It sometimes made them very angry, and it sometimes made them very sad, and it sometimes made them very rude to other people, and it sometimes even made them hit other people, just because someone they had never met, who was wearing a T-shirt in a different colour to the one they liked, had kicked a ball in a net.*

But that's the thing – we act in these ridiculous ways because football means so much to us. Because my football club will be the one constant thing in my life until the day I die – you lose friends, partners and family, but the football club will always be there (hopefully). I just wish they'd win something occasionally.

Read All About It

The young man looked up and peered into the sky as he approached Canada Square, Canary Wharf, and saw the impressive headquarters of the Daily Mirror newspaper. It had come a long way since being founded in 1903, as a newspaper for women, run by women.

He made his way to security, obtained a pass, and ten minutes later, found himself in a small training room with about ten other people.

A man with a loud voice was stood at the front.

"Welcome everyone. Thank you for coming today. I hope it will be an enlightening experience for all fo you, and thanks for volunteering for work experience at the Daily Mirror."

"We like to do things differently around here, so before you get to see the place in action, I thought we could do a little quiz, to see if you lot have what it takes to work for this newspaper."

He walked round the room, handing out pieces of paper.

"It's multiple choice in part, open questions in other parts. Twenty minutes. Off you go…"

Twenty three minutes later……

"So you want to work for the Daily Mirror? Well, let's see how you did on our test. This will tell us a great deal as to whether you have what it takes to work for this fine and noble institution."

"The test we used today was a themed one. The topic on some of the questions was Manchester City football club. Always a club that generates great debate. Let's see how you did."

"The first section of the test was about headline writing. I gave you a scenario and you had to come up with a headline. The scenario was this:

Manchester City announce a reduction in season ticket prices for the following season. What headline would you accompany with this story?"

"Some interesting ones from you here…."

CITY COURT FANS WITH PRICE REDUCTION

CITY WOO SUPPORTERS WITH CHEAPER SEATS

"Hmmmm. Not quite what we were looking for…let's see…ah yes….here's a couple that have got the right idea…."

CRISIS CLUB CITY BRIBE ABSENT FANS WITH TOKEN GESTURE

CHEAPER SEATS AT TEMPLE OF DOOM AS CITY BEG FOR SUPPORT

"Liking that one. Well done Simon."

Simon smiled.

CITY FLAUNT WEALTH DURING CREDIT CRUNCH

CITY USE VAT REDUCTION TO TRY AND APPEAR GENEROUS

"Bit wordy that one, but your heart's in the right place."

"Anyway, an interesting start, let's move on."

"Scenario two: The paper is short on stories. We need to fill half a page the following two days. Do we:

a) Put in an opinion piece about FIFA, and then one about the FA.

b) Trawl world football despatches for some stories.

c) Make up a story linking Manchester City to a world-class player, then lead the following day with his rebuttal*."

*or "shunning", as we like to call it.

"The answer was of course C. Seems to have a stumped a few of you, this one."

"You have to be careful of course. The Sun don't seem to do a good job of this."

 He brought up a powerpoint slide on the screen.

Manchester City have categorically played down suggestions that they are mounting a £100million bid for Barcelona superstar Lionel Messi. Dr Sulaiman Al-Fahim, who was believed to be a board member at Eastlands, stated "Messi is a player that makes me love Argentina again." leading many to believe City were preparing a big-money raid on Camp Nou for Josep Guardola's prized asset.

However, City have stated Al-Fahim holds no position at City and that the story linking Messi, who has rebuffed talk he wants to leave Barca, with the club are untrue.

"Following an article in The Sun newspaper which claimed that Manchester City are preparing a £100m bid for Lionel Messi, the Club would like to make the following information clear," read a statement on the club's official website.

"The story is untrue and this fact has been accepted by the newspaper in question. General comments about Lionel Messi, made by Dr Sulaiman Al-Fahim, who holds no position at the club, were mistakenly linked to Manchester City. "The article was printed in error and an apology to His Highness Sheikh Mansour, Chairman Khaldoon Al Mubarak and Dr Sulaiman Al-Fahim and a correction in Saturday's edition of the newspaper will follow."

"Of course, we have to print the odd apology when the teams get a bit uppity, but we can hide them in the depths of the paper where no one will notice them. A bit of false contrition, and off we go, the cycle starts again. We print many stories over the course of a year, mistakes are bound to happen."

The young man put his hand up.

"Didn't the Mirror have to apologise to City for claiming Micah Richards had handed in a transfer request?"

"Yes I believe so."

"Didn't you recently have to apologise to Nicklas Bendtner for misquoting him?"

"Yes, unfortunate incident."

"And to the regiment you accused of torture in 2004?"

"Yes, that is well-documented. We were duped by some very skilled con artists."

"And to Bryan Ferry, who you accused of singing the praises of Nazis?"

"Yes, yes, we have had to make a few apologies, like any newspaper."

"And to Kate Middleton after she complained of harassment in 2007?"

The man with the loud voice glared at the young man. If looks could kill.

"And haven't you had to apologise to Prince William too?"

"Is there a point to all of this?" the loud man bellowed.

"And to Josh Hartnett a few months ago, paying him substantial libel damages?"

"Shut up!"

The young man got a crumpled piece of paper out of his pocket.

"And to Andrei Shevchenko? And Roman Abramovich. And his ex-wife? And Natasha Kaplinsky for claiming she doesn't clean up dog poo? You also stated: "We were wrong to report that Sam Griffiths was drunk when he was electrocuted running across railway tracks at Burgess Hill, West Sussex, in the early hours of New Year's Day, or that he had drunk five cans of beer. The coroner at his inquest concluded that Sam and his friends were "merry as you might expect . . . but not the worse for wear from drink". We apologise for any distress caused to his family and friends... and on May 6 under the headline "Grease chiefs hit by pounds 8k Gest list" we said that David Gest had made a string of backstage demands before agreeing to appear on the show including a DVD of himself being played in his dressing room together with various refreshments served at specific temperatures and chauffeur-driven cars for his friends. In fact, David did not make any of these demands which, we have now discovered, were circulated as a hoax by an unknown person and we apologise to David Gest for publishing them.""

"Enough! Let us move on."

The young man folded the piece of paper away.

He thought it best not to mention David Anderson, a journalist writing for the Mirror, who last year repeated a claim deriving from vandalism on Wikipedia's entry for Cypriot football team AC Omonia, which asserted that their fans were called "The Zany Ones" and liked to wear hats made from discarded shoes. The claim was part of Anderson's match preview ahead of AC Omonia's game with Manchester City, which appeared in the web and print versions of the Mirror, with the nickname also quoted in subsequent editions on 19 September 2008. The embarrassing episode was featured in Private Eye.

The loud man appeared flustered. He tried to compose himself.

"Now, onto Question 3 – we gave you a quote, and asked you to make a story from it. This is a true test of a journalist – footballers quotes are almost always bland and uninteresting. It is our job to spice them up.

Garth Barry's quote was:

"The way we've played this season, there's no reason why we can't get enough points from the last eight games to be there or thereabouts (4th place). Anything after that, I'll deal with at the end of the season.

"It's not the be-all and end-all playing in the Champions League, but it helps in a World Cup year playing at the top level."

"Some good answers from you all, but not quite sensational enough. This is the headline we actually went with."

'Barry fuels summer signature scramble with top-four blast'

"We then went on to insist Gareth is so "desperate" for Champions League football he'll quit Villa to get it if need be."

"Simples."

The man with the loud voice wandered over to the desk at the front of the room, and perched himself on the corner.

"Now, I need to say a quick word about how times have changed in the world of journalism over the past couple of decades. Long before the credit crunch came along, all newspapers had to start cutting costs. No more regional correspondants and offices across the country, we have had to get the news sent to us, cut down on staff, and use news wires and, if I am being honest, by "utilising" other stories."

The young man thrust his hand in the air again.

The man with the loud voice sighed.

"You mean plagiarism?"

"I mean, we all help each other out in these difficult times. The news is out there to be reported by anyone."

"Anyway, this brings us onto Question 4."

"David Anderson a valued colleague of mine, was told to write a story on Ronaldo, for the next day's edition. David didn't have anything to hand. So what does he do?

a)   Re-print an old article

b)   Scour the new wires for some news

c)   Try and contact Ronaldo for some thoughts

d)   Read ZOO magazine, copy an interview in there, and slap an EXCLUSIVE tag on it.

"Another question that caught most of you out. The answer was D, read ZOO magazine."

"Here's a few bits from David's article"

"I like people whistling and booing!" Ronaldo said. "It's normal for fans to do that. There's nothing I can do and it doesn't matter anyway.

"I have to concentrate on the game, so I don't think about that sort of thing. On the pitch I'm a target, but it is difficult to avoid these things. I don't believe that people want to hurt me on purpose. In my experience, the game just doesn't happen that way. Truthfully, I've never had any serious problems."

"Dave of course reveals his source during the article, which, is only fair. But I think he has done a good service by letting the wider public hear the thoughts of one of the world's top players."

The young man put his hand up again.

The man with the loud voice frowned. His two eyebrows became one.

"My, you are inquisitive aren't you?"

"The Daily Mirror's Darren Lewis was on Sky Sports News this morning, and said "Coloccini, £10m pounds, struggles to hold down a place." " This would be Fabrizio Coloccini, who has started each of Newcastle's 30 league games this season."

"Yes, well, as I have mentioned, we work under a lot of strain here. With resources and staff cut, there just isn't the time to do thorough research on the odd occasion."

"But surely your football reporters do watch the occasional premiership match?"

"Yes of course. They are extremely passionate about their job."

 The young man put his hand down, smiling wryly as he did so.

"Now finally, I'd like to talk to you all about an extremely entertaining programme on Sky called the Sunday Supplement. We send the occasional journalist on there, and it is a great way to pick up tips on how to approach the issues of the day, and hone one's skills. "

"Watch how the Sunday Supplement manage to belittle City so effortlessly. We can learn a lot from them. You link City to a world class player. There doesn't have to be any truth in the rumour. There rarely is. Then you can spend five minutes saying why would any player go to City, would only go for money and so on. It's so easy!

We don't have to leave the office anymore! Having a foreign owner makes it even easier!

As for the Glazers however - well they have shown how foreign owners should run a club. We'll ignore the £600m of debt. We're not in the business of upsetting the big clubs, espcially the biggest, best and most glamorous club in the world.

Journalists have become so ingrained with the idea now that United are the pinnacle of everything football-related, that they can appear on the Sunday Supplement and sit there with a straight face questioning why anyone would possibly choose Real Madrid or Barcelona over Manchester United. We can learn a lot from them."

The young man put his hand up in the air.

The man with the loud voice could contain himself no longer.

"What now?! What is your problem?!!! "

"Sorry, it's just that I feel the need to point out they do tend to talk a lot of nonsense much of the time. I mean, last week Patrick Barclay said that Ben Foster was the best young keeper in decades. He said that Real Madrid would struggle to get in the top half of the premiership. No one took him up on this."

"Yes, but…"

"Last week's motley crew spent 20 minutes telling Capello what squad he should pick for the World Cup. I mean the guy only won four serie A titles as a player, and the Coppa Italia twice. And seven Serie A titles as a coach. And the European Cup, various domestic cups, La Liga twice, Serie A coach of the year…."

"Yes, yes, yes, we get the message!"

"Then Matt Lawton stated that Real Madrid were at the lowest ebb in their history - an opinion formed entirely on 2 games against liverpool. (conveniently ignoring the 11 consecutive wins before that)."

"Enough!"

The man with the loud voice grabbed the young man and frog-marched him out of the room.

The young man continued talking to the end.

"Your wonderful reporter Michael Calvin decided last week in some pathetic article that Robinho was on £250,000 per week. How do you sleep at night making this c**p up?!!......."

The door slammed shut.

The young man was being given a quick tour round the building before he went. The man with the loud voice wanted him thrown out, but apparently he had a right to the tour, so the tour he would have. The old man, with 40 years at the paper, was showing him the main office.

"Why are there Christmas crackers lying around everywhere?"

"Oh, Derek McGovern uses them for his articles."

The old man showed him into his little office.

"I have to deal with correspondence from the public."

"What does that entail?"

"Usually, putting letters through the shredder. Look at this article from Oliver Holt. He got a lot of replies to it, not surprisingly."

I felt guilty last Saturday evening. Because Manchester United played a few miles away from where I live and I didn't go to watch them.

I listened to the commentary of their FA Cup tie against Fulham at Craven Cottage on the radio as I drove my daughter to a swimming pool in north London. The pangs got worse.

The commentators were raving about United. They were ransacking their minds for new superlatives. It sounded as if they were watching football poetry by the Thames.

Not that it's anything particularly new praising United. Sir Alex Ferguson's sides have dominated the game here for the last 15 years.

There have been great teams to watch, filled with great players. Too many to mention, really. A cast of stars.

But it feels as though there's something special about Ferguson's latest creation, as though what he has built at Old Trafford has taken another step forward in its evolution.

The way this United team play football, you want to take your kids to a game so that in years to come, they can say they saw them play.

Whoever they grow up to support, they can say they saw a United side that was chasing five trophies.

They can say they saw Ryan Giggs in his glorious autumn, Wayne Rooney growing into his prime, Cristiano Ronaldo in his pomp, the fiery majesty of Paul Scholes, the breathtaking passing of Michael Carrick and one of the best English club defences there has ever been.

And they can say they saw Ferguson himself, standing watchfully over his charges in his Old Trafford perch, gazing down at his final achievement and the one that we may yet remember him by.

For all those reasons, it will feel like a privilege to watch United take on Inter Milan in the second leg of their Champions League second round tie this evening.

Seeing them take on Liverpool, the pretenders to their throne, on Saturday afternoon will be equally unmissable.

It's possible, of course, that Inter will spoil this script by beating United tonight. How typical of their boss, Jose Mourinho, it would be to conjure a result like that.

But the evidence we have seen so far suggests that won't happen. The evidence we have seen so far suggests that Inter, like most other teams, are simply not in United's league. United were so much better than Inter in the first half of the first leg at the San Siro that the gulf was embarrassing. Inter were lumpen. United were brilliant.

Apart from all the individual talents the team possess, what is so striking about this United team is its technical accomplishment.

There is nothing traditionally English about their style at all. They have travelled a million miles, too, from the 4-4-2 orthodoxy that ruled their fantastic Treble-winning side of 1999.

They are fluid now. So fluid they slip through your fingers. So fluid they're close to perfecting Total Football. Very close.

Their close control is fantastic. They play the ball into feet at pace into tight areas. They keep possession. They pass the opposition to death.

Their movement is like quicksilver. Players such as Rooney and Dimitar Berbatov, dropping deep, pulling wide, are unmarkable.

Their speed of passing and their speed of thought is reminiscent of the Spain team that outplayed England so comprehensively last month in Seville. And compliments don't come much higher than that.

So I hope United wipe the floor with Inter tonight. Not because they're English and Inter are Italian.

But because this United team represents everything that is good about the game and Inter don't. And because their quest for five trophies is something to be marvelled at, even if, sooner or later, it may come unstuck.

If you can get a ticket for anything in sport, get a ticket to watch this United play.

The old man passed a letter across his desk.

"We got this reply a couple of weeks later. I am just about to put it through the shredder, once I have emptied it out. "

Having read your inspiring article, I felt I just had to see this amazing team! So I got tickets for their next two matches – Liverpool at home and Fulham away. Time to see more football poetry, and create new superlatives.

New superlatives eh? They must be better than the Brazil 1970 side, the Holland side that created "total football", the Hungary side that ran rings round England. To say I was excited is an understatement.

And I took my two sons as well, Seamus, 8 and Christiano, 6. They were so excited. Seamus bought a Ryan Giggs pencil case to take to school, and Christiano had his Carlos Tevez duvet set, though admittedly he has been having a lot of nightmares ever since.

I have to say Mr Holt, I was rather under whelmed with what I saw. In the Liverpool match, the other team seemed to be a lot better, and the United players kept hitting the ball to the wrong place, falling over, and fouling the opposition.

Against Fulham, they were even worse. Their manager went purple with rage! They couldn't pass to each other, there was a red-headed guy who thought he was playing volleyball, and they sure seem to moan a lot. Petulance is the word I am looking for. Do you really think this is what I should be showing my kids? I'd rather set a good example to them than let them think that harassing referees and crying like a baby when things don't go your way is the right thing to do.

Wayne Rooney growing into his prime? What was he like before??

Christiano Ronaldo in his pomp? Just looked like a whinging, spoilt child to me.

Fiery majesty of Paul Scholes? On the aforementioned volleyball court maybe. Total football? He can't tackle, I know that much.

My children were full of questions:

"Dad, why is that old man always chewing gum?"

"Dad, why is that young man so angry? Why has he just punched the corner flag?"

"Dad, what's a granny-shagger? Dad, what's a prostitute?"

"Dad, why do the team in red keep shouting and arguing with the man in black?"

"Dad, why are they singing about Hillsborough?"

I had no answers.

I thought maybe Alex Ferguson could give me some after the game, but apparently he doesn't speak to the BBC. To hear his thoughts I would have to subscribe to the club's own TV channel.

I recall you saying in a previous article that you are a Stockport County supporter. I read in the news last week that this fine club is in danger of going bankrupt, and thus out of business altogether. 126 years of history, soon to become but a memory. Surely you would be setting a much better example to your children if you took them to see their local team, the team their father supports, a team desperate for support, rather than whichever team is doing the best at the moment? Just a thought.

This United team represent everything that is good about the game at the moment? Don't make me laugh.

"He talks a lot of sense"

"Yes, I guess so."

"How long have you worked for the Mirror?"

"Oh a long, long time young man. Many decades. I've seen many changes. Nothing is like it used to be."

The old man struggled to his feet, and walked slowly to a cupboard, where he retrieved a large scrapbook that he brought back to his desk

"Have a look at this. It's very interesting. Some headlines from down the years. The paper was originally a very genteel and uncontroversial affair. However, in the late 1930s it transformed itself from a gently declining, respectable, conservative, middle-class newspaper into a sensationalist left-wing paper for the working class that soon proved a runaway business success."

The young man was mesmerised. He flicked through some early headlines

First up was 1904 – City had 13 players in their Cup Final squad. A player called Livingstone, a Scottish "laddie", had a touch of influenza, or "some such trouble". The City half-back Ashworth was suffering from rheumatism.

Under the headline MANCHESTER WIN 'T' COOP, City won the cup for the first time, and Bolton took their defeat "very quietly".

Several of their footsore supporters were not in such an equable frame of mind. There were several very spirited battles of words on the grassy slopes just after the match. The Manchester men were known to "crow" over their victory, though no punches were thrown.

The players were overwhelmed with anxiety to play their very best. The lightning-like movement by which Meredith got round Struthers was what caused the pen and ink critics of the game to boggle.

Then he found some snippets from 1923 – and a record crowd assembled at City's "palatial" new ground to witness them defeat Sheffield United 2-1, due to a strong showing after the "breather".

He noticed an advert for Craven "A" cigarettes, made specially to prevent sore throats.

1933 next, and a match report talked of gate receipts of £4697 as City won at Everton. Everton beat City in the Cup Final however, though Geldard was described as "downright bad".

After the 1934 Final, he read that Frank Swift fainted from the exertion of it all.

It was all so straight-forward and civilised. The headlines stated the facts – who won, how, who excelled, who didn't.

He flicked forward to recent times, and compared the early articles with the modern Mirror headlines.

WAN CHEWS SICK TOFFEES

KEE-GONE

DROP DEAD GEORGIOS

CITY MAKE EMILE OF IT.

It certainly had all changed.

The old man spoke some more.

"Since the 1960s, the story of the Mirror has been one of almost continuous decline. By the mid-1970s, the Sun had overtaken the Mirror in circulation, and in 1984 the Mirror was sold to Robert Maxwell. The import of heavyweight columnists and writers with a following, like Paul Callan from the Daily Mail, sat uneasily with the perceived need to compete with The Sun. After Maxwell's death in 1991, a period of cost-cutting and production changes ensued. The Mirror went through a protracted crisis before ending up in the hands of Trinity Mirror in 1999, and in recent years, the paper's circulation has also been overtaken by that of the Daily Mail. Nowadays, ratings are earned by sensationalising everything, and grabbing the attention of your working-class man. It doesn't sit comfortably with me, I have to say. We even tried to get rid of the red logo for a short while, using a black one instead, to try and get away from that sort of reporting, but we were fooling no one. The red logo was soon back. We are a red top, pure and simple."

The young man stood up and shook the old man's hand.

"Thanks for showing me round."

"It was a pleasure young man. You take care."

He left his pass with security, and made his way outside. He met up for a drink with a friend in a nearby pub.

"So, what was it like?"

"Not for me, I don't think."

"That's a shame."

"Yep. Think I'll stick with banking after all."

Burn Him

(names have been changed to protect the guilty)

The father tucked his young son into bed.

"What story would you like tonight, son. Perhaps a comic? Or how about a legend from not very long, long ago?"

The boys eyes widened!

"A legend please dad!"

"Ok, son. And when I say legend, I should point out that this story is entirely true. Only the names have been changed, to protect the innocent."

"Ok!"

The young child took a sip of his Carlos Queiroz cocoa ™.

"Not very long, long ago, there was a man called Manuel Adebuy-your. Manuel was from a small country a long way away called Tango. He used to play football for a team called Arsenal Wanderers, but they booed their players a lot, so he moved to a new club called Madchester Rovers, who had lots of money, and liked to brag about it."

"Did everyone hate them dad?"

"Yes they did son. They had no class, and no history, unlike their neighbours across the road, who had all those things, and a quiet dignity and humility that all the gold in Abu Derby Doo could not buy."

"They sound horrible!"

"Oh they were. Anyway, Manuel got to play against his old club. Another player, called Van Persil, tried to hurt him so nasty Manuel kicked him in the head as he slid by. This made the other team mad. Then Manuel scored a goal and celebrated in front of the mad team's fans. This made the mad team's fans mad. They threw stuff at Manuel, including certain items of fruit, but we won't mention that again."

"Madchester Rovers won the game, but the other team were very bad losers, so they started crying and their biggest cry baby of all, Van Persil, made a statement on the club's website saying how hurt he was by the challenge. This player had previously been sent off for kicking an opponent in the head and walking up to a goalkeeper and elbowing him to the floor."

"What's a website dad?"

"It's what people used to use to communicate with each other before humans developed mind-reading abilities."

"It sounds rubbish dad."

"It had its uses. Anyway, soon Sky Sports News got hold of the story."

"Wow dad, were they around a long time ago?!"

"Yes son, though they weren't owned by Manchester United in those days. Not officially, anyway."

The father chuckled.

"Now Sky were under the thumb of the 'Big Four' Football clubs – Arsenal Wanderers, Madchester Etihad, Kidneypool and Chelski. The last thing they wanted to do was upset the most powerful clubs, so they had decided that the kick by Manuel was the worst in the history of football, which began in 1992."

"Worse than Alan Shearer's kick on Lennon?"

"That was an accident son."

"What about all Rooney's kicks at players dad?"

"If you took out his passion for the game, he would have been half the player. So those kicks had to be put into context son."

"What about when Chris Morgan fractured the skull of the Barnsley player, almost killing him?"

The father was impressed by his 6-year-old son's detailed knowledge of legendary footballing incidents.

"The referee booked him son. You can't go charging players afterwards and undermine the referee. Well, unless you play in Sky blue of course!"

The father laughed. The son frowned.

"Anyway, Sky decided to run with the story for the rest of the week. They called it a stamp, even though it clearly wasn't. They showed the foul every ten minutes, from multiple angles. They wheeled into the studio endless ex-referees, managers and ex-players to condemn Manuel. They even interviewed the FA Chairman who condemned the tackle. He just happened, by pure coincidence to support Arsenal Wanderers."

"That doesn't seem very fair, dad."

"Life isn't son, life isn't. Well, unless you're in the Champions League every year, then life is very fair indeed."

"Anyway, by Monday the witch hunt continued, and now the possible ban was up to 10 matches. Maybe even prison. I mean, if he'd done that in the street…"

"Don't be silly dad!"

"Some people actually think like that son. During all of this, there had still been no mention of Van Persil's goal celebration, his lunge on Adebuy-your that resulted in the alleged stamp, or the Arsenal Wanderers players spending the match trying to hack Manuel down, including three attempts during one mazy run."

"Why was that dad?"

"It's to do with agendas son. When you're older, I'll explain in more detail."

"Ok."

"You see son, the Wanderers fans booed their own players quite a lot, so there was no reason not too after they had left, and they hated Manuel because he had courted another team called Intra Melan. Fabbygas himself had courted a team called Barcyloner every summer, but that was ok with the fans of the Wanderers."

"Now, it wasn't long before the Premier League chief executive, a Mr Dick Scoobymore, had his say as well. You see son, Madchester Rovers had already been accused of killing football. And now individual players were killing it too, according to Dick. He said: 'We've had a fantastic two days of football, and that includes the game at Eastlands. Why then, when you run the Premier League, would you want the headlines on Sunday through to Monday being something else? You don't want it, do you? So clearly it doesn't do any good for the brand that is football in one sense. You'd rather it didn't happen. Of course when these instances come up you'd rather that the talk was about the action and the goals.'"

"Dick couldn't see the irony of how him talking about it even more was simply exacerbating the situation."

His son nodded his head. He had no idea what exacerbated meant though.

"Soon, the police were involved, what with Manuel's terrible, riot-inducing goal celebration and all that. Former Met Police commander John O'Connor said: 'I am sure the police will want Adebuy-your to be made an example of. From a police perspective, Adebuy-your could have been arrested and then charged with actual body harm for the incident with Van Persil. He would then have faced the prospect of standing trial in court.'"

"But dad he never touched anyone!"

"Don't worry son, remember, this is just a story!"

"Oh, yes. Ok!"

"No one would actually say that!"

"But dad, wasn't he booked by the referee at the time. Shouldn't that have been the end of it?"

"Of course son. The rules were quite clear on this. Under the FIFA Laws of the Game, The FA is prohibited from taking disciplinary action when incidents are seen at the time by the match officials.

An FA spokesman once said: 'The Football Association can only take action in the case of incidents that are not seen by officials.

"Whilst it is clear that the officials did not see the full extent of the incident, they did see players coming together and to take any further action would be tantamount to re-refereeing the game and this would be contrary to the laws of the game.'
And thus son when a Mr Bosingwa kicked a Mr Benayoun in back - no charge. When a Mr Rooney kicks opponents? No charge. When that nasty Mr Barton karate kicked Etuhu - no charge. You see, they had a nice little get out clause whereby the referee could say he dealt with it at the time, or he could say he didn't even though he obviously did, so that the player could be charged."

"So dad, the police would ignore the behaviour of the Arsenal fans, and all sporting precedents in rugby and football, and waste the public's money in bringing a prosecution against a footballer for running along a pitch and then sliding on his knees but would then walk free as any case would involve reasonable doubt being easily established, something that the FA do not bother themselves with in their 'Kangaroo Court'?"

The father patted his son's head.

"Well done – you're a quick learner! And such a wide vocabulary for a 6-year-old!"

"Everyone wanted their say though, son. There was a journalist called Simone Hattenstone, who ridiculously claimed to be a Madchester fan. He said "If even now all he wants to do is take out his revenge with his studs and provoke crowds into riots what's he going to be like when things go bad?"

Ex-player Raymond Parlour said "Adebuy-your really owes Arsenal something for bringing him up", even though he had appeared in champions league final squad before then, as if

Arsenal were some sort of charity who signed players out of the goodness of their hearts."

"That's probably why they never won anything dad!" The child laughed.

"Oliver Holts compared it to Cantona's kung-fu moment. Alan Greene said the book should be thrown at Adebuy-your - having admitted he hadn't seen the incident. Allies though came from the strangest of places. That horrible nasty man Raymond Keane stuck up for Manuel and even Patrick Barclay said 'Fans lose their right to be offended when they go on the offensive. If they cannot take it — these miserable products of a sick society who consider a player's family fair game for the vilest insults and yet, because of their numbers, are allowed to continue to serve as football's audience — they should not give it."

"Stan Collybore said Manuel should have got a 2 match ban for the goal celebration alone. Bobby Gouldd said that the whole affair would lose England their World Cup bid. These were worrying times."

"But anyway, he got a three match ban – City reluctantly accepted it.And that is the end."

The father turned the page over, and was about to close the book....

"Oh, hang on, it wasn't..."

"Come Thursday and the press had moved onto his foul on Fabbygas. Sky showed super-slo-mos of it from 15 different angles for 2 days. Soon other incidents were mentioned. Now he had slapped Songe, and it was feared that it wouldn't be long before an altercation in the tunnel involving a ball boy and the theft of his pocket money suddenly came to light to add a couple more games to his ban. And still there was no condemnation of the Van Persil lunge, or the three players that tried to cut Adeby-your in two during his mazy run."

"The opinions kept coming. Manchester United legend Alexandre Stepney believed Emmanuel Adebuy-your got off lightly with a three match ban. 'I seem to remember George Best got a six-week ban in 1970 for knocking the ball out of a referee's hands so I think Adebayor did get off lightly. These incidents are more noticeable nowadays.' You couldn't argue with logic like that, son."

"So was that finally the end, dad?"

"Well, almost son. Manuel still had to be punished for the goal celebration. You see an Arsenal player had done the same thing in front of their biggest rivals Tottingham Warmspurs just a few years previously. There had been no outcry, or punishment, because the Warmspurs fans had decided not to riot. In the end, Manuel got a nice little fine, and a suspended ban."

"And that's the end, dad?"

"Very nearly. Well, not quite. Henry Vinter, another pompous journalist out of touch with the real world, felt the punishment was nowhere near severe enough. He said: 'So whose emotion do you want most in football? A multi-millionaire itinerant footballer crowing in the face of erstwhile employers who nurtured him, paid him handsomely and cherished him until he was tempted away by riches elsewhere, or fans momentarily allowing their passions to run away with them in defending their club? Thursday's decision by the Football Association not to punish Manuel Adebuy-your for inciting Arsenal supporters at Middle Eastlands on Sept 12 is devoid of logic, defies police evidence and makes a mockery of its chief executive's stance. The case of Adebuy-your versus Arsenal forms part of a broader debate about player-fan dynamics. The Madchester Rovers forward's defence was that he had been pilloried by Arsenal fans and had a right to be emotional when scoring against them. In return, Arsenal supporters argued that Adebuy-your, painfully unprofessional in key moments, such as the Champions League semi-final last season, had shown a lack of respect to the club that helped make him. Adebuy-your's subsequent contemptuous comments about Arsenal, particularly the fans, inevitably heated the emotions of those entering the away section of Middle Eastlands. Just as every village has an idiot, every support harbours some unpleasant types, yet anyone with any experience of travelling around the nation's many grounds will agree that Arsenal's following is one of the less threatening.Some yobs rushed to the front, faces disfigured with hate, as Adebuy-your celebrated his goal in front of them and Arsenal can certainly do without them. But Adebuy-your is paid to be there, and with that comes responsibility.

Footballers being human, allowances must be made for the intoxication of the goalscoring moment (which is why the petty rule of a caution for removing a shirt should be scrapped). From Marco Tardelli's screaming to Ryan Giggs's hairy chest and Lee Sharpe's Elvis impression, great celebrations should be, well, celebrated. But Adebuy-your crossed the line. He even crossed the halfway line in his 70-yard run to goad the Arsenal fans. In every sense, Adebuy-your went too far. A one-game ban would have reminded him and his immature peers of that. It's not difficult. Carlitos Tévez showed with his respectful approach to West Ham United fans last week, a contrast to Adebuy-your.The gut instinct of the FA's chief executive, Ian Watmore, that the governors' "Respect" campaign demanded players show some self-control was correct. Sadly, Watmore has been undermined by his own organisation. Gay Neville, so often the scourge of FA officials, was unintentionally to blame. Red Nev's Sept 20 taunting of Madchester fans was a far less splenetic offence, hardly requiring of more than a warning, yet his escape set a precedent, allowing Adebuy-your to follow him over the wire. The FA has stupidly stoked the home fires for Adebuy-your's visit to the Emirates on April 24. Now that will be emotional.

"But dad, anyone with a brain knows West Ham fans like Tevez!"

"Yes son, anyone with a brain. Unfortunately in times of legend, the people paid to write tended not to engage their brains first. And then we come back to agendas. But that is for another time."

The father tucked his son up in bed, and turned off the light. As he left the room, his son said:

"Dad, what happened to Madchester Rovers in the end?"

"Well son, they became very successful. The people in the press had to change their attitude, because of their success. And their fans finally saw some trophies come to Middle Eastlands."

"And did the club find some humility and dignity?"

"No son, money can't buy you that."

Much Ado About Nothing

Commentators. I have a theory about them – I think Kenneth Wolstenholme has got a lot to answer for, and it's his fault that I dislike so many of the current crop.

Wolstenholme's "they think it's all over" quote from the 1966 World Cup final was a spur of the moment comment that gained international fame, book deals, was sampled in hit records and even got its own TV show.

Wolstenholme had previously been established as the BBC's authoritative voice of football and went on to cover the climax of five World Cup championships and the finals of 16 European Cups and 23 FA Cup finals besides dozens of internationals.

He was proud that he had produced a timeless piece of broadcasting and coined a phrase that has entered English folklore. But this was tinged with a hint of regret that the words had overshadowed the rest of a hugely successful and ground-breaking career (though he used the phrase for title of his memoirs, so wasn't too upset, clearly).

Over on ITV, Hugh Johns was the "the other voice" of the 1966 World Cup final. At the same moment, to a much smaller audience, Mr Johns was concentrating more on the striker's hat-trick as he told ITV viewers: "Here's Hurst, he might make it three. He has! He has... so that's it. That is IT!"

I like Johns' commentary. It does the job for me. The problem is no one remembers his words. And now every commentator wants not his Johns moment, but his Wolstenholme moment. It seems sometimes that every commentator wants fame, and a legacy of a piece of beautiful prose at a key moment in a key match. And no Clive Tyldesley, anything to do with "that night in Barcelona" doesn't count. So rather than comment on what's happening on the pitch, commentaries have become a competition to see who can say the most dramatic, prose-soaked comment. I am still scarred by a Portsmouth match commentated on by Peter Drury at the end of last season, where Drury felt it apt to continuously refer to Portsmouth's financial problems by quoting Shakespeare. It was the best of times, and it was the worst of times, you see!

Oh hang on, that's Dickens.

But as Piquione volleyed in the second goal, I thought to myself that it was a far, far better thing that he did, than I have ever done; and I couldn't help think that it was a far, far better rest that he went to than I have ever known.

Drury would have worded it so much better though.

"What can Portsmouth do in this second half? If football be the food of love, play on. To sleep, perchance, to dream, for the Pompey fans have discovered that all that glitters is not gold. O coward conscience, how dost thou afflict me, and Utaka's missed an absolute sitter there! Lord, what fools these mortals be. Thoughts, Craig Burley?"

"Well, youse got to say he should've buried that, the lad's gonna be disappointed not to hit the target."

A new breed of commentators emerged a few years ago, each of whom seemed to have their own "angle". Commentating well was deemed not to be sufficient anymore.

For Drury this meant prose and intellectual nonsense, Alan Green's was to criticise everything, and Jonathan Pearce's "angle" was to SHOUT VERY LOUDLY about everything. Because even a throw in early in the game had its own little frisson.

I prefer him now that he has calmed down – another blogger said he now sounds suicidal, but he doesn't irritate me anymore, so he must be doing something right.

Now I have no problem with commentators doing research before a match - they should be doing, it's their job, not that this has concerned studio pundits or many co-commentators. What I can't stand is the need to crowbar statistics in, and more than that, the need to crowbar puns and catchphrases that they have been working on, as if they have just completed a six-week tabloid headline writing course.

Jonathan Pearce has said that 90% of his job is research, but only 2% of that will be used during a match. That's how it should be. Less is more.

It wasn't all this way – it's easy to get nostalgic, but Davies, the old Motson or Wolstenholme did not attract the ire that their modern counterparts do. Or maybe that is just a result of modern media whereby anyone (even me!), can broadcast their views to anyone who will listen. All you had in the old days was Barry Took on Points of View (I've lost half of you now).

And John Motson used to be good, before he became a celebrity (fancy a fridge magnet with Motty quotes on? It's on Amazon if you do). Now he is the uncle on Xmas day sat in the corner dozing after one sherry too many. I don't know if it's just me, but his Match of the Day reports seem to have been recorded after the event. Tyldesley is nothing more than a sycophant, mainly for Manchester United. Armed with a box of tissues, each of his match commentaries is nothing more than an exercise in idol worship, whatever the score or however United performed. This is not an anti-United comment, it's anti-Tyldesley. He supported United home and away in the 70's, and you cannot just throw off your allegiances, football does not work like that, his prejudice is plain for all to hear.

And then there's Alan Green. Now it's very fashionable to have a go at Alan Green, so that's what I am going to do. Where do I start on this odious, vile, ego-driven man?

Now he has his supporters of course, who argue quite simply that he is one of the few commentators to "say it as it is". I am not sure what they mean by this, but presumably, looking at the evidence, they mean he whinges, moans and criticises everything before him. So in other words, they think football is rubbish. Well he certainly seems to think so – if he does enjoy the beautiful game, he certainly hides it well (hypocritical maybe as all I am doing is moaning too, but if I was paid to watch football I'd cheer up in no time).

At the Champions League final, for which he was being paid handsomely to watch, his first thought was to moan about how awful the commentary position was.

For an England international, within three minutes of the match kicking off he had moaned about the weather (sorry we couldn't sort that out for you Alan), the new England kit, banners around the edge of the ground (he doesn't like them, like most things), and two attempted tackles/passes by England players.

I have never known a man suck the joy out of a football match like Alan Green does. I have never known a commentator so full of himself, with such a monstrous ego.

And all this would be ok, or at least more acceptable, if he was prepared to argue his corner, to stand up for what he believed in. But if you have had the misfortune of listening to 6-0-6 when he is host, you will know that criticism of anything he has said is not allowed. He repeats outright lies and when questioned on them claims "it's only my opinion". Lies are not just opinions. There is a difference. One such example I can recall involved Nicklas Bendtner, where Green spent much of the show slagging off quotes attributed to Bendtner where he seemingly exaggerated his own talents. Shame Green had ignored Bendtner's subsequent press release that week saying he had been totally misquoted.

This is a man who in his tedious Belfast Telegraph articles has stated he doesn't like Manchester City (and thus shouldn't be allowed anywhere near the ground, in my opinion), spent a year slagging off everything our Brazilian players did, and staggeringly criticized Sam Allardyce for the size of his ego!

Pot, meet kettle.

It's all subjective of course, but even I know there are good commentators. Generally those that stick to describing the action, give you a rounded-picture of the match, and keep matters in perspective. I've no doubt it is not an easy job, but it can be done well. What I don't need to know, because I don't care, is what the commentator thinks about City's wealth, banners around grounds, Mexican waves, football kits, the weather, managers, the price of tuna in supermarkets or the quality of hamburgers at Villa Park. I'll form my own opinions, thanks. You're there to describe the match Alan, so why not give it a go? And whilst you're at it, go and read your employer's charter, especially the bit on impartiality.

As for co-commentators, the less said the better. Usually they tend to be those who have played the game, so bearing this in mind, where has all their experience and expertise gone? Mark Lawrenson's approach seems to be to nothing more than to tear open a few Xmas crackers and memorise the jokes. Putting the pun in punditry but not bothering to try.

The comments follow the same road with co-commentators - I've seen them given, he'll be disappointed with that, the manager will want more from them in the second half, blah blah blah…churlish perhaps to criticise such comments as they have ninety minutes to cover, but a bit more depth would be nice.

Other sports fans are spoiled with their analysis. Why can cricket, Formula 1 and rugby for example enjoy such great commentary and analysis but football can't?

And do we even need co-commentators? They appear to add nothing. I recall a match last season when a co-commentator had taken ill and the main commentator (may have been Motson, not sure), had to do the match on his own – and the whole commentary was better for it. Not only was the co-commentator not missed at all, but the main commentator seemed to perform better when flying solo. It seems many commentating teams have little chemistry or rapport, and just seem to drag each other down. And as for David Pleat – some say he brings much tactical analysis to the table, most of which must have been on nights I had the telly turned off, but irrelevant of that, how can a co-commentator be employed who CANNOT PRONOUNCE PLAYERS' NAMES?!

But despite Green, radio seems to have got it right more than television. Radio 5's football coverage is generally excellent, and it is TV that seems to struggle. With radio commentary, you are required to stick to the script and describe what is happening, as you are the eyes. With TV, commentators seem to think that silence is evil, and must not be allowed. I couldn't disagree more. You could turn the sound off, but then you'd lose crowd noise too.

So I would argue that the memorable moments, on and off the pitch are spontaneous moments that cannot be rehearsed and planned in advance. Going back to that glorious day, and it got me wondering how Drury would have covered that 1966 World Cup Final finale.

"And here comes Hurst, sprinting up the pitch. Could this be it? Jeff Hurst, ask not what England will do for you, but what together we can do for the freedom of man! Let every nation know, whether it wishes us well or ill, that we shall pay any price, bear any burden, meet any hardship, support any friend, oppose any foe, in order to assure the survival and the success of liberty! Goal!"

As for Alan Green?

Green: "Some people are on the pitch. Oh this is disgusting, absolute disgrace. Ban them for life, no one wants to see this, animals, what are they thinking, shame on you, shame on you! I am embarrassed to be British, this is shocking, are they looking for a fight, they might be, idiots, absolute idiots, oh dear oh dear, ruined the game for me, shocking."

Jimmy Armfield: "Hurst has scored by the way, 4-2, hat trick for him, England have won the World Cup!"

Green: "Have they? Oh but it's been overshadowed for me, it really has...oh, and now everyone's doing a Mexican wave, they really should be shot."

Hugh Johns had the right idea.

Commentators And Their Separate Law Book

The other Sunday the entire nation (according to the man's man Richard Keys) watched Tottenham Hotspur v Manchester United. Super Spectacular Sunday or something, or maybe Dull Derby Draw Deadlock D-Day. But going back to the Spurs game, I think we can all agree that surely a game of this importance shouldn't be settled by a sending off?

No? Well Jonathan Pearce thinks so. And he said precisely that as United were reduced to 10 men.

I am clearly being lazy – I have obviously missed the rule change brought in by FIFA that stated that laws change according to the importance of the game. Or maybe the law has always been in place and I am just really stupid. Or maybe Jonathan Pearce is an idiot. It's one of the three (maybe more).

It also seems appropriate to ask what stature of game Pearce considered the match to be – at the end of the day (my cliché of the day) it was Tottenham Hotspur v Manchester United. A big game, an interesting game for the neutral and both set of fans alike (or so I thought), but it's hardly the World Cup Final. It was 5th v 2nd (1st by end of play).

It's the same liberal application of logic that sees commentators bemoan referees sending off players very late in a game, instead preferring that they used a "bit of common sense", or commenting that a red card had "ruined the game as a spectacle", as that's the last thing we need – afterall, it's a sad day when applying the laws of the game correctly is more important than entertaining the masses.

Tony Cascarino once commented, as he discussed Ronaldo's red card against Manchester City a couple of years ago.

"It's a red card, but I just wish, for the sake of entertainment, that referees used common sense sometimes."

Here's a suggestion - why don't commentators accept when commentating that the referee is there to apply the laws of the game, not turn a blind eye. Afterall, it is not just a case of commentators not knowing the laws, more that often they think they should be liberally applied. Or again, maybe it's me. Maybe I missed the announcement that stated that contact with another player is automatically a foul. Or the rule that a player who raises his hands is automatically risking violent conduct and thus can have no grounds for complaint. Or the agreement that deems acceptable a commentator's analysis that he has "seen them given" when judging a penalty appeal, as if this has any relevance to the situation.

Applying common sense is a quite idiotic mantra to push. No two people have the same idea of what constitutes common sense – and as I have said before until I am blue in the face, it is not the referee's job to be doing that anyway but applying laws. Of course, there are extenuating circumstances occasionally. A slippy pitch should be taken into account when assessing some tackles, a feisty derby may require a different approach from the referee, but throughout, the laws of the game never change.

One of the biggest cries is "all we want to see is consistency" and I think I can help here. I had a good ponder about this, I even thought outside the box for a while, and I think the solution is to let one single referee do every Premiership game. This way, we will get consistency. Yes, I know there's a few logistical problems with this approach, and no two games could be played at the same time, but instead of focusing on the negatives, let's look at the positives. Total consistency, and the same standard of refereeing for everyone. I see no downside.

Referees are human beings. As if every referee can apply the laws and assess situations the same. It just doesn't work like that. There are areas where consistency is needed – for example handball by a defender jumping in a wall at a free kick. And referees need a more consistent approach to issuing red cards, as there is too great a discrepancy amongst them. But in other areas total consistency is nigh-on impossible.

It has been this way for a long time with commentators and pundits alike. Take Andy Gray, who also seems also to think that laws shouldn't be applied all the time. We can go back as far 2006 to see an article of his for football365.com, when he penned a scathing piece on Graham Poll after he sent off James McFadden. The gist of his argument can be summed up in this extract:

You would have thought that Graham Poll would have kept his head down this week, taken himself out of the firing line and made sure he wasn't involved in any controversy that would put him on the back pages again.
He must have known that his every move would be under scrutiny after the weekend, that anything he did would be open to question because of the reactions of the Chelsea players - so you would think that he would have avoided any contentious decisions on Wednesday night.
If referees sent players off every time they gave them a volley of abuse, every other game would be abandoned. It's a passionate and emotive sport where the fear of failure means that anger is always bubbling just below the surface ready to explode if you feel like you've been treated harshly.
This is not a modern phenomenon. I swore at the referee all the time and I'm hard pushed to think of a player who didn't, even the supposed nice guys of the game. Anyone who thinks foul language can be eradicated from the game is barking mad.

What Andy Gray is basically arguing is two things. Firstly, that a referee that has had a tough week, or given some controversial decisions recently, should keep his head down and not make any more controversial decisions. Andy Gray thinks he should not apply the rules as he sees fit, and call decisions the way he normally would, but chicken out and turn a blind eye. Secondly, he comes out with the moronic argument that football is a passionate game, and swearing at the referee is a natural consequence of this passion. By his logic, as football is the only sport where referees are treated in this way, then football must be the only game with any passion. I mean, I've never seen ANY passion in a game of rugby or cricket.

This is the one other area I think we do need to see consistency – punishing abuse from players - it will soon stop.

The irony is that a commentator can joke about women not knowing about the offside law while sitting in the studio every week showing themselves to have a crass ignorance of the laws, and fellow commentators can spend years talking about a daylight rule when deciding offside that never existed as more than general guidance and was dropped years ago anyway.

At the weekend, these same arguments raised their head once more. Frederic Piquionne put West Ham 2-1 up late on in the game against Everton then was sent off after his over-exuberant goal celebration.

Chris Kamara on Goals on Sunday was not impressed with the referee, stating that he could have shown some of that famous "common sense" and let him off, especially as it was his last season as a referee, so sod the assessor in the stand. Andy Cole nodded his head in approval. Of course the referee was entirely correct to send him off – he was doing his job. It's a stupid law in my opinion, but a law nevertheless. The referee acknowledged this by shaking Piquionne's hand as he sent him off – he knew he had no choice.

And throughout this, who has escaped any blame? Why, Piquionne of course. Reinforcing the old stereotype that footballers are thick, he jumps into the crowd whilst on a yellow card. Of course it appeared to be a vital goal, and he was overjoyed and keen to celebrate – but it is possible to do this without jumping into the crowd. Only one person was to blame for that dismissal, and it sure as hell wasn't the referee, yet still people are quick to blame him. Unbelievable, Jeff.

Maybe I was the only person speechless at Mark Clattenburg ignoring a blatant penalty for Chelsea at the end of the Blackpool match last September because it was 4-0 and the match was about to end, and he would have had to send a player off. Maybe I was the only person nauseous at him laughing with Drogba and then high-fiving and hugging him.

Maybe it was just me. I mean, he was only applying a bit of common sense.

Is Waving An Imaginary Yellow Card Really That Bad?

There were plenty of metaphorical pats on the back for Rio Ferdinand last week when during the Spurs v Manchester United match he told Rafael not to wave an imaginary yellow card at the referee, as this sort of behaviour was not tolerated. Foreign players with British clubs have been berated by team-mates before when doing this, as happened with Fabrizio Ravanelli and Mikel Arteta in their first seasons in the Premier League.

It seems that in this country, waving an imaginary card at the referee is akin to serial killing or questioning a woman's knowledge of the offside law.

This is nothing new. In October 2005, the Daily Mail ran a campaign to rid the game of this "evil".

Players will be told to cut out the imaginary card-waving to encourage referees to book a rival as part of the drive to rid football of the problem.As Sportsmail's campaign to punish the perpetrators drew support from all parts of the game yesterday, the FA Premier League is taking steps to address the issue.

Referees' chief Keith Hackett will ask PFA chairman Gordon Taylor when the pair next meet to remind his members of their responsibilities, not only to the game but to each other.

Hackett will also stress to Taylor that refs already have the power to book players for waving an imaginary card and that the pre-season agreement for more respect towards officials from players and managers is being compromised.

Graham Barber, who retired as a Premier League referee in 2004, said: "I'd like to feel that if cautions were introduced, it would act as a deterrent with clubs telling their players to stop doing it. But if this was introduced, it would be up to everybody - clubs, players, managers and the media - to support referees.

Former West Ham striker Tony Cottee also backed the campaign. Now a Sky Sports pundit, Cottee said: "Those players who do this should be booked. Absolutely. I've been saying it for two or three years since it came into England. Action is long overdue. When a player waves an imaginary card, the referee should say: 'Yes, it is a yellow card, but it's for you'. It's just unacceptable, trying to get a fellow pro into trouble. It's the referee's job to decide whether a foul deserves a yellow card."

In 2006, there was talk from UEFA of ensuring a similar clamp-down. That paragon of virtue John Terry has moaned in the past about Barcelona players doing it.

An article in When Saturday Comes touched on the same theme last year.

There is nothing that annoys football commentators more than seeing players wave an imaginary card after they have been fouled. Jonathan Pearce, Peter Drury and co seized on such displays during the World Cup with weary despair. Some of the things imported into British club football from abroad in recent times are tolerated – over-elaborate stepovers and wearing undershirts displaying messages for God are just about acceptable – but the card mime is beyond the pale.

Of course the card waving is gamesmanship, just like stealing a few yards at a free-kick or claiming a throw-in that you know is for the opposition. But you can see why it developed when teams get away with blatant thuggery as Holland did during the final.

The thing I don't get is this: a large percentage of players spend games trying to con the referee – why does this particular action get so much attention?

Is it the horror it provokes at trying to influence the referee? Or the idea that there is nothing lower than trying to get a fellow professional dismissed, or at least punished with a yellow card?

The waving of the card is just one of a hundred ways that players will try and influence the referee or his assistants during a match, other methods often involving out and out cheating.

In every match we see gamesmanship throughout. Where's the uprorar about leaving a trailing leg? Commentators will be apoplectic about waving a yellow card, but it's considered "professional" to "win" a free kick.

Or appealing for throw-ins or corners when the player knew they touched it last. This must happen thirty times a game. What about feigning injury (my personal pet hate)? Or specifically feigning injury as a time-consuming tool? Or the goalkeeper taking the goal kick on the far side of the goal to waste those extra few seconds. Taking two minutes to take a throw-in. A player knowing they're going to be substituted and wandering over to the far side of the pitch so it takes so long to walk off the pitch most of the crowd have lost the will to live.

Or how about moving the ball forward at a free kick whilst the referee isn't looking? Or similarly, edging the wall forward a few inches at a time. And so on, and on, and on.

Like diving, there is this conception that card-waving is a trait brought into the English game by those nasty foreigners. Maybe that is why it is raised on a pedestal. All the tricks of the trade we Brits have already mastered are not seen as bad.

Spitting has a similarly bad reputation – now spitting at or on someone is pretty gross, no doubt about it, but I'd prefer to be spat on than elbowed in the head or be scythed down by a leg-breaking challenge.

The answer may also lie in our eyes – what we see is greater than what we later hear. By which I mean that the waving of the card is a very visible sign of a player trying to influence the referee and get an opponent punished. It is seen as worse than the player telling the referee he should book him.

When Wayne Rooney was sent off for sarcastically clapping a referee, it emerged that referees had been instructed that this was seen to be worse than being swore at by a player as it was a more visible sign of dissent. And thus, so is the waving of the imaginary card, but referees don't seem as keen to clamp down on this.

Referees of professional games are themselves professionals, and should be making decisions without being swayed by the actions of the players after the event. The waving of the card shouldn't matter in changing the outcome of anything, but admittedly it is naïve to think referees are not swayed by the reactions of players.

The "card mime" is not something I like to see - I don't applaud it or remotely support it, but to me it's no worse than a hundred other things going on in a game. Perhaps if other offences were seen in similar light, the next time a United player dives Rio Ferdinand will give him a piece of his mind. I wouldn't hold your breath.

Winter Breaks

It's that time of year again. As Spain's footballers go on their holidays until the second weekend of January and other countries follow suit, here in Britain the traditions run deep and rather than rest, the football authorities cram in as many games as possible, with Premiership games for six consecutive days around the New Year, which sees yet again having to play twice in three days, with the small matter of three big cup games and another five league games to squeeze in too. Only the Portuguese league carries on throughout outside British shores.

As a nation we are genetically designed to show disgust at the thought of a mid-season break. It goes against everything we stand for, and games every two hours is part of the festive season, as traditional as Santa Claus, turkey dinners or vomiting in dark alleyways after a Xmas do.

This is a game of the fans, and the fans benefit from wall-to-wall football. The players are paid £200,000/£400,000 a day/minute/week, so they should stop complaining. It's a squad game too, so managers should use their squad. Agreed?

I've always held a fairly similar view, but there is serious evidence to suggest that a break benefits players. This is especially true when there is a summer tournament for players to prepare for. So don't complain when Wayne Rooney breaks his metatarsal in March – it's all your fault. You, the consumer. It doesn't matter how much they are paid, how primed they are as athletes, how good their club facilities and physios are – it is logical to give players rest occasionally. It is not just a case of players picking up injuries later in the season through fatigue – but it's also an opportunity for players to shake off niggling injuries they've been carrying through the season – a common occurrence (City have at least one player currently performing with such a concern). With harder and poorer pitches at this time of the year, injuries become more likely, a point Alex Ferguson has made in the past. A UEFA study 10 years ago showed discrepancies in the injury rates of leagues that did and didn't have winter breaks. I don't think I need to point out which leagues had more injuries. There's even some stats that suggest that after a winter break, teams score more.

Of course there is one big problem of having a winter break, even if you agree with the principle of one – when do you have it? It is currently a barmy 12 degrees (centigrade) outside, and will continue to be mild for the next week at least. In previous years it has been minus nine and I walked to work across a frozen canal. There is no way of knowing how the British weather will pan out over a single week, never mind a whole season. The packed Christmas schedule shows that the FA already struggle to fit in all the games that are played over a season – if we had a winter break it would make things near-impossible. If we had a winter break then hit a bad spell of weather, it would be utter carnage. If we were to have a break, there would have to be fewer games – it's really that simple.

Martin O'Neill recently advocated a break, but he sees it from a different angle – that the effects of a break can be psychological, not just physical. O'Neill said: "My personal view is that I would love to see it happen, even for a week or two because psychologically, I believe when you start off the season, it's pretty long and it gives you something to think about during that time. Even if it was only for a fortnight, I think psychologically, it would help everyone - that's my view. When we were in Scotland, I experienced it twice in the five years I was there and one of those years, Celtic reached the UEFA Cup final. I didn't think it was a coincidence myself."

It's not surprising that many managers want it. Sir Alex Ferguson wants it. So does Fabio Capello. Capello's logic should be obvious – he wants a fresher squad come the summer, rather than a group of players who have mostly exhausted themselves after a gruelling nine months of non-stop football. Simon Kuper's *Why England Lose* also cites the lack of a winter break as why English players are generally more run down and prone to niggling injuries come summer tournaments.And back in 2004, the then FA chief executive

Mark Palios told the BBC that a league winter break was the target, but his words were ultimately empty.

The break may well never happen in England. With so many games to play, there is simply no room for manoeuvre. Even if there was a break, in a game where money rules, many teams would probably take advantage by arranging high profile foreign friendly games anyway. Unless Leagues reduce in size or the Carling Cup bites the dust, it seems nothing more than a pipe dream. And if the fans demand entertainment over the holiday season, do they not come first?

The Obsession With Attendances

I was at the Manchester City v Newcastle match earlier this season, shaking my head at the Newcastle fans' ridiculous chants of "where were you when you were s**t?", whilst crowing about empty seats – all this from a club that used to pull in 15,000 crowds and had 10,000 empty seats just the previous week. Isn't it ironic - don't you think?

But then the thought occurred to me. Why the obsession with full houses and attendances anyway?

There are huge swathes of fans who wear their club's attendances as a badge of honour, or report with glee when rivals' attendances dip a couple of thousand. Manchester City fans will point out the attendances when we were in the third tier of English football, Manchester United fans will point out they had the highest attendances in the old days too, those dedicated Newcastle fans pack out St James Park every week, and so on.

Of course loyalty is an individual trait, and fullness of ground depends also on capacity and catchment areas and pricing structures and the traditional wealth of the fans that would attend, the opponents and so on....and global recessions of course.

You could argue that the more home fans there, the more support for the team, which aids results (though anomalies historically have shown the odd team to suffer badly under the pressure of playing in front of their own). For the owners of a club, every seat brings extra revenue, but for a premiership team, the odd thousand here and there makes up a very small percentage of total revenue.

Attendances in the old days used to vary wildly, week by week. Most games didn't sell out. A team would get 15,000 one week, then 50,000 the next. On September 8th 1948, Manchester City v Birmingham City drew a crowd of 26,841. Three days later, 64,502 watched the Manchester derby. A dip into the archives reveals some startling attendances, and results. And games on Christmas day too (up to 1976 in Scotland, though weather prevented that last set of fixtures. It was 1959 in England, with just two games played).

Martin Samuel wrote a a couple of months ago about how "Chelsea should have exploded in Abramovich's time, making a move to bigger premises essential".

Samuel continued: " He (Abramovich) has done everything right. He has invested substantially in players of good quality, who have in turn delivered success. He has encouraged entertaining football, and 44 goals in 11 games this season suggest an ambition fulfilled there, too.

He even froze ticket prices for four years prior to this season, equating to a net deduction of 15 per cent, with inflation considered. So what is Chelsea's problem? Strangely, there isn't one. They are simply proof of how incredibly hard it is to grow a club organically beyond its traditional size.

Arsenal moved from Highbury, where the capacity at closure was 38,419, to a new stadium at Ashburton Grove holding 60,355, and filled it instantly. Yet Arsenal have long been established as the biggest club in London and at the time of leaving Highbury had a 20,000-strong waiting list for season tickets, closed for some time. This, in part, prompted their move. The board knew that, in essence, Arsenal were a club with a following of 60,000; it was just that 22,000 of them couldn't fit inside the stadium.

Chelsea continue to look at plans to expand, but without the enthusiasm that exists elsewhere. Their big leap came between 1989 and 2003 when the average gate rose from 15,957 to 39,770. They hit the 41,000-mark the following year and have remained there since. "

So, success brings crowds, which is logical, but there's only so far it can help the figures. Cost is hugely important to restricting growth in attendances in recent years – just look at the Bundesliga attendances to see what can be achieved with a sensible pricing policy.

But success of course makes the casual supporter more likely to attend, and the inevitable glory hunter contingent to emerge from the woodwork. Arsenal had an average of 24,403 fans in 1992-93, but the average had risen to 38,053 by the 1997-8 season. Manchester United had an average at the end of the 1980s of 36,474, which had risen to 55,168 just 8-9 years later. From 1992-98 Everton found 15,000 new fans on average, Wimbledon doubled their attendances, as did Chelsea.

This does not tell the whole story – the 1990's of course followed the 1980's, and the 1980's was a low-point in match day attendances. Poor facilities, hooliganism, and tragedy went hand in hand to put people off in their droves. The ugly spectre of Thatcher and ID cards are the abiding images for many of that period. The only way was up once Sky got involved, and football was polished, preened and placed on a pedestal.

I've heard it said many a time that teams like Wigan don't deserve to be in the Premiership, as the people of the town can't be bothered going to watch them anyway – this to me is drivel – you don't earn premiership survival by the size of your crowd. Wigan deserve to be there as they got fairly promoted, and pick up enough points each season to stay there – end of. They have fans that attend matches regularly like any other club, just less than many of their rivals. They might not add as much as others to Sky Sports' super-duper best league in the world viewpoint of the Premier League, but that doesn't relinquish their right to be there.

The question is, what will happen now to crowds? There is some evidence that gaps are beginning to appear in the premiership more and more – but the brand is strong, and even though many clubs continue to raise prices above the rate of inflation, the crowds will continue to come, in the lower leagues too.

A report a year ago of English football crowds suggested they were on course for a 50-year high if ticket sales in that season were maintained across the nation's four professional divisions. An initial forecast by sportingintelligence was that total gates in 09/10 would be in the region of 30.4m people. That would be higher than at any time since the 1959-60 season, when 32,538,611 fans streamed through the turnstiles. Burnley won the top division that year (then the First Division), while the runners-up, Wolverhampton Wanderers, lifted the FA Cup. Aston Villa won the Second Division (now the Championship), while Southampton won the Third Division (now League One, where the Saints again reside). Walsall won the Fourth Division.

Between then and the 09/10 campaign, only one season in English football has seen total crowds go above 30 million, and that was in 1967-68, when 30,107,298 people paid to see Football League matches. Other reports had suggested this rise would not happen, as fans were increasingly being put off by increasing costs on match-day – ticket prices, refreshments and all the other costs that attending a match entails. Many interviewed even suggested watching lower league football instead as a cheaper alternative.

Attendance figures continue to suggest that these fears are unfounded however. Many a time over the last 15 years I have considered not renewing my season ticket and picking my games, but I never do (and probably never will). And as if to prove that fans continue to attend in droves, last year's attendance figures for the three football leagues did indeed hit a new 50 year high. To put the growth of the Football League in context: total crowds in those three divisions alone last season were higher than all four divisions in England combined at the game's low point in 1985-86, when just 16.49m people came through the turnstiles. For now, the future is still bright.

The Final Thoughts

City's failings used to matter too much. A City defeat would ruin a whole weekend, a big problem when the team you support is distinctly average, often worse. At some point, I had to take a step back and try and accept my team as one of life's bugbears, and try not to let it spoil everything. Getting a season ticket helped, once I discovered the wonderful world of credit cards in 1999. Then you get to appreciate the other aspects of supporting your team. The craic, the friendships, the shared misery, the cost of Just For Men. But what else would we do with our lives without football? What other activity could possibly have given you the feeling you experienced on 13th May, just before 5pm?

Nothing.

I think Manchester City have done something miraculous. I think they've removed my pessimism for the club. It was pessimism so deep-routed that five years of extensive therapy would barely have touched the surface. But by somehow pulling through this season, by exorcising so many demons over the past year or so, it may have gone, for now.

Maybe.

May 13th was the day that men were allowed to cry. Even men with tattoos and scars and stuff. Not me, not at the time, I was too busy trying to breathe. In the end it was something so obscure that set me off. A comment from a Celtic fan on a youtube video about the last five minutes of the premiership season. A short, simple comment about how happy he was for City fans, how we deserved it, and how it had caused joy to people all over the country. Damn that pollen count once more.

I'm not sure if I am a glass half-empty sort of person because of City, or I chose them to suit my outlook on life. Maybe it's a new era for both of us.

It's good to win things. As I said right at the start, I didn't choose my team because I thought they would be really successful – it was the last thing on my mind as a 7 year-old. City just felt right. My dad is a United fan, and took me to both City and United. Living in the depths of Whitefield, there'd be plenty of trips to Gigg Lane too. But City just felt right – the cobbled streets and terraced houses, the stands looming large as you turned the corner, the misshaped stands, the blue kit, the feel of a fallen hero looking to get back on its feet. It ticked all the boxes. And if I had known how long the wait for some tangible form of glory would be, I would probably have walked away. Patience, hope, expectancy, can only last so long. But it was worth the wait. It's always good to win something, to bask in a reflected glory with those you are close to, to walk into your place of work with your head held high, with a sense of achievement for something you contributed nothing to. A football club is one big family, and any family needs something to smile about every now and then. The one thing I do know is that the arguments about buying the title, oil money and lack of class are tiresome and flawed – whatever the circumstances, I know that this piece of success over the past few years has, for many tens of thousands of City fans, been fully earned. We kept the faith.

Long may it continue.

Printed in Great Britain
by Amazon.co.uk, Ltd.,
Marston Gate.